A Catholic Soul Psychology

Randolph Severson

A Catholic
Soul Psychology

Foreword by Robert Sardello

GOLDENSTONE PRESS | *Benson, North Carolina*

Published by Goldenstone Press
P.O. Box 7
Benson, North Carolina 27504
www.goldenstonepress.com

ISBN: 978-0-9832261-7-8

Cover artwork: Cornelius Sullivan, *Saint Michael The Archangel*,
oil on canvas, 30 x 40 inches, 2010, collection of the artist
www.corneliussullivan.com

Cover and book design: Eva Leong Casey / Lee Nichol

Printed in USA

GOLDENSTONE PRESS

GOLDENSTONE PRESS seeks to make original spiritual thought available as a force of
individual, cultural, and world revitalization. The press is an integral dimension of
the work of the School of Spiritual Psychology. The mission of the School includes
restoring the book as a way of inner transformation and awakening to spirit. We recognize that secondary thought and the reduction of books to sources of information
and entertainment as the dominant meaning of reading places in jeopardy the unique
character of writing as a vessel of the human spirit. We feel that the continuing
emphasis of such a narrowing of what books are intended to be needs to be balanced
by writing, editing, and publishing that emphasizes the act of reading as entering into
a magical, even miraculous spiritual realm that stimulates the imagination and makes
possible discerning reality from illusion in the world. The editorial board of Goldenstone Press is committed to fostering authors with the capacity of creative spiritual
imagination who write in forms that bring readers into deep engagement with an inner transformative process rather than being spectators to someone's speculations. A
complete catalogue of all our books may be found at *www.goldenstonepress.com*. The
web page for the School of Spiritual Psychology is *www.spiritualschool.org*.

10 9 8 7 6 5 4 3 2 1

For Sally—

what we've shared and what we've built

CONTENTS

❀

ACKNOWLEDGEMENTS

This book crowns something. For their long vigil of support, my wife and family, daughter, sons, granddaughter, grandsons are deserving of more than I can return. So, too, my parents, long departed, and my brother, Craig, and sister, Joy. I wish to give special thanks to Dr. Robert Sardello, for his gracious foreword, and also for the Wisdom and Kindness he has shown to so many, for so long, including myself. To my friends and colleagues, Drs. Charles Fischer and Robert Kugelmann, Father Robert Williams, Carol Demuth, James Gritter, and Mary Ann Cohen who have sustained and understood my need to go on, and on, I am deeply grateful. My gratitude extends as well to Mr. Lee Nichol, whose care and detailed artistry completed a very ragged, fragmented vision; to Jocelyn Chafouleas who has helped bring so many of my excursions into final form; and to Eva Casey for her design of the cover and layout.

I wish to thank the Doctors and Guides, living and dead, whose presences are as compelling to me as their books; together with my patients, who are also teachers, brothers and sisters-in-arms who have shared with me, and I with them, so many defeats and victories on the Fields of Life. Sing, Muse, all of them. Finally, as ostentatiously pious as it might sound, I give thanks to God, the Father, the Son and Holy Spirit. Every day I thank my Lucky Stars that I am Catholic.

FOREWORD

I feel privileged to introduce, very briefly, this book by Randolph Severson. Brief, because the tone and style, the erudition and insight, the level of truth that unfolds, the extreme importance of this Catholic psychology, can only be diverted by any excessive attempt to employ conventional introductory language. And, any attempt to try and even come close to the level of what you are about to read would be false. Alongside the rhetorical abilities of this author, usual narrative writing immediately shows its inherent deficiencies, particularly with regard to the focus of this book—a Catholic soul psychology. Logic and coherence can too easily take the place of action and presence in writing, because the former is our habitual way that writing keeps us distant from ourselves and enables readers to keep distant from themselves. It is better, by far, to limit to the extreme this usual way, and invite you to enter into the action that is this book.

We are taken, right at the start, into the action of creative and fruitful rebellion! We never think of counseling as political—and even cultural—rebellion, but then psychology typically centers on what is "wrong," and how it can be corrected. And, the "correction" always throws the individual into the middle of the habits of a culture that can no longer be correctly called "culture" at all, captured as it is by a kind of introverted totalitarianism. That is to say, becoming free of loss, sorrow, trauma, confusion, and all the rest—the reasons people go into therapy—means being re-integrated into a life of complete control by the forces of materialism, seeming to offer whatever we desire, while removing what is most centrally desired by the soul—inner freedom leading to outer creativity; and the essence of freedom is to be able to orient soul, heart, and practical life,

XII • A CATHOLIC SOUL PSYCHOLOGY •

consciously, to seeking the Divine, not just on Sunday, but as our primary joy of life.

This book is not a psychology written by someone who happens to belong to the Catholic faith, nor is it the imposition of Catholicism and promotion of it within the field of counseling and psychology. Any stance for or against Catholicism needs to be held in suspension in order to let the work here do its work of re-awakening deep—perhaps the deepest—values inherent to being human.

I do not feel the book is "about" anything—not in the sense of the kinds of writing and words we are used to, the kind of spectator consciousness within which an author of a psychological work remains asleep to the soul even while speaking of soul. Here, there is no difference between what is written and the action of soul itself. The soul's presence as author-presence does not remain hidden. We as readers are actors within the soul's battles rather than spectators seeking yet more information, or worse, verification of where we are already inwardly culturally located.

Through the many strong flourishes herein—speaking the nature of psychology, the nature of the human soul, the nature of suffering, the nature of specific values, of tradition, of true individuality—you will feel all these dimensions and qualities actually awakening within you because they are present *in potentia*, that is, present in their coming-to-be. Every value, what the human being can be, is always present; these invisible, archetypal, and prototypal dimensions do not "go away." In fact, the author forcefully puts forth the proposition that so-called psychological difficulties are human crises that can—if heard rightly, responded to with soul-empathy—lead to something more than comfort from fear and alleviation of distress, and that such alleviation is in fact the announcement of entering, with joy, the large battles of life.

When what can therapeutically be heard are the cries of a person in battle for soul rightly conjoined with world, then what is called for is courageous leadership and correct strategy, leading to victory, restoration of the inherent spiritual orientation of the soul, and the utmost dignity of being human—the capacity to locate ourselves, rightly, within the unknown, but very present divine guidance. The role of the counselor, within this vision put forth by Randolph Severson, is nothing less than the strategist and leader of the embattled soul to its victory.

Verification that it is indeed possible to go so deep as to undermine the deadliness and superficiality of pseudo-culture—and that our sufferings are not intended to drown us in suffering, but are in fact the Way into being human—is provided over and over with stories of the greatest of us, from ancient to modern individuals. These individuals discovered the life of enduring but buried truths of the human soul, and stepped into courageous action to defend these truths—intellectually, practically, within wars, within work, within family, within the Church.

What breathes through every pore of this writing is freedom: freedom from blind obedience to what we think we are, to what we think we want, what others and the world want us to think about who we are. Such habits of obedience are shaping a world in which we will no longer wish to live. A person seeking counseling has, with great fortune, come to this abyss, but with great misfortune, is often therapeutically treated in such a manner that what brought them to the abyss is never really discovered; superficial personality diagnosis and treatment is accepted as the role of psychology. Re-forming personality inevitably means "adaptation." It is something entirely different to work to bring personality-nature into harmony with human-nature. This aim is relentlessly pursued in this book, in multiple ways—intellectual acumen and honesty, stories, personal history, directives concerning what constitutes counseling as the presence between two people of the Wisdom of the human being. Each section of this writing unfolds one of these forms so that every aspect of the soul—our thinking, our feeling, and willing—is intimately addressed.

Robert Sardello, Ph.D.
May, 2013

Introduction

What follows are three essays in homage to Freud and Hillman—or, rather, one rather longish essay, a story that bodies forth in spiritual, emotional vision what I merely sketch out here, and a series of prose poem-like reflections. These essays are an attempt to articulate a psychology that is at once rooted, traditional, worldly, soulful, spiritual, archetypal, psychological, and Catholic; a psychology that is also a psychotherapy; a sacred psychology dedicated to St. Michael, and whose patron Saint is St. George. "All the Angels and Saints"—we Catholics regularly recite this phrase. The air is awash with Angels and the Saints go marching in. St. Michael: St. George.

Saint Michael and Saint George, the guardian angel and protectors of the Popes and the Kings of England. The Angel who appeared in the cave in Italy, Monte Sant'Angelo, where, tradition has it, the "Other Conquest"—the Norman conquest of Sicily and Italy and nearly Constantinople—began. Legend has it that on May 5th in 493, a herder hunting for a lost bull discovered him in a deep dark cave. Failing to catch him, the herder shot an arrow at the bull, which stopped in mid-flight then came back to wound him. Rushing home he told his Bishop, who ordered a three-day fast and then returned to the cave. "Scarcely had he arrived before the Archangel Michael appeared in full armor, announcing that the cave was henceforth to be a shrine to himself and to all the angels. He then vanished, leaving behind as a sign his great iron spur." To this cave through the centuries came Popes and Saints and Kings, one of whom, Otto III, walked barefoot there from Rome. And then a band of Norman pilgrims: "whose conversation with a curiously-dressed stranger in that very cave changed the course of history and led to the foundation of one of the most powerful and magnificent kingdoms of the Middle Ages."

And St. George, the Roman Tribune and Martyr who would not renounce his faith, and who appeared over the battlefields of World War I, leading English soldiers into battle.

I have worked at this project for over forty years. I have been a practicing therapist for thirty, a solo practitioner for twenty—a clinician, if you will, who has chafed and bristled at the inexorably advancing secularization of our discipline, its denial of the soul, of the spiritual, of the sacred. "Professionalization" has left us with nothing to profess. Diagnosis has first replaced and then aborted phenomenological description. Contracts in which a client gives an informed consent for treatment have replaced a covenant between an I and Thou.

Nonetheless, throughout this time I have chosen to wear a hair shirt, so to speak—to remain within the tradition of psychology, to live and think and to live and think it through, to be a professional therapist, while at the same time serving and proving worthy of the soul, of the spirit, of sacred influences, of all the Angels and the Saints, especially St. Michael and St. George. "To take upon ourselves the mystery of things / as though we were God's spies," as is said in *King Lear*. Whether this book completes and justifies this project the reader must decide. But it has been what I have taken to be my calling, my vocation, or as Reinhold Schneider would have described it, my commission. St. Michael. St. George. "Oh air pride, plume here / Buckle! AND the fire that breaks from thee then . . . O my chevalier!"

PART ONE

A CATHOLIC SOUL PSYCHOLOGY

Prologue:

Catholic Archetypal Psychologist

The prince, as generous metaphor for responsible citizen and concerned member of the polis, will keep a focused mind, a mind undistracted by the multiple diversions of peace, and a psyche neither numbed nor in denial. And he will maintain this clarity not merely by meditating or praying to benefit his own "mental health," but for the common good and the defense of his community. Hence the prince "ought never let his thoughts stray from . . . war."

—James Hillman, *A Terrible Love of War*

During his development Freud went through an unmistakable militaristic phase, which he traced ultimately to the battles with his nephew in early childhood. One of the first books that fell into his childish hands after he learned to read was *Thiers' Consulate and Empire.* He tells us how he pasted onto the backs of his wooden soldiers little labels bearing the names of Napoleon's marshals. His favorite one was Massena, usually believed to be a Jew; he was aided in his hero worship by the circumstance that they were both born on the same date a hundred years apart. The Franco-Prussian War, which broke out when he was fourteen, aroused his keen interest. His sister relates how he kept a large map on his writing desk and followed the campaign in detail by means of small flags. He would discourse to his sisters about the war in general and the importance of the various combatants. His dreams of becoming a great general himself, however, gradually faded . . .

—Ernest Jones, *The Life and Work of Sigmund Freud*

Writing books for me is anyway much like a military campaign. I confess to fighting my way through with military metaphors. There is a strategy, an overall concept, and there are tactics along the way. When stuck, don't dig in; keep moving forward. Don't obsess trying to reduce a strongpoint by sheer force or laying siege. Isolate it and in time it will fall by itself. No pitched battles with the interior voices of saboteurs, critics, adversaries. A light skirmish, a shower of arrows, and disappear into the next paragraph. Camouflage your own vulnerability, your lack of reserves with showy parades and bugles—remember everyone else is vulnerable. Pillage the storehouses of thought, refurbishing old material and use it to reinforce your lines. Abandon ground you can't exploit, but when you've got an issue on the run, take all the territory you can.

—James Hillman, *A Terrible Love of War*

Catholic archetypal psychology. The Catholic part of my title is largely self-explanatory, although there is ample room for interpretation, disagreement, even sharp divide. But when someone describes himself as "Catholic," most people feel that they have been told something and that, essentially, they understand what is meant. The meaning of Catholic in this context should become progressively clear as I proceed.

The archetypal psychology part requires a definition of terms. C.G. Jung introduced the idea of archetype into psychology. One of Jung's most succinct definitions is: "archetypes are the forms or river-beds along which the current of psychic life has always flowed."[1] The concept, however, cannot be confined to Jung. It derives from the Platonic conception of ideal forms. As a specific term, Augustine first employed it. In fact, in developing the idea Jung essentially reflected the fascinations of his times. From Burckhardt to Madame Blavatsky, from Fraser to Creuzer, from Steiner to Guenon, in the studies of the scholars and in the lecture halls at German and Swiss universities, in London drawing rooms, in French Masonic halls, like the Ancient Mariner's water, mythic archetypes were everywhere, "about my table to and fro / the elemental creatures come and go." Karl Jaspers compels us here, while leveling trenchant criticism at Jung:

> What Burckhardt termed "archaic images," Klages termed "images" and Jung "archetypes." But there are certain essential differences between Klages and Jung. Klages' interpretation has a fascinating vividness. His presentation of the symbols of poetry and art remains as perhaps the really lasting contribution in all his great work . . . Jung on the contrary lacks the impressive vividness of Klages and his work has nothing like the same weight. He is the deft master of all the means of interpretation but the inspiration is missing . . . Jung's expositions become tiring and irritating because of his many undialectical contradictions. As the reader emerges from many of Klages' pages, he is struck by a winged quality which is lacking from the work of Jung who favors a worldly skepticism. The present day is poor in symbols and both these men are anxious to discover primary reality. Jung's efforts strike me as a fruitless new start through the exploitation of what is old . . . [2]

Whether Jaspers' dismissal is just (I would maintain in one way it is not, for it is precisely Jung's "worldly skepticism," his eccentricities and earthiness, that redeem rather than disqualify his work, redeeming it at times from his own and many of his followers' sterile preoccupation with the grandiosities of gnosis), Jung was not alone in his quest for "primary reality" nor in his intuition that the architecture of such reality could be known and described through the concept of primal forms. "Presences that passion, piety or affection knows" (Yeats), "the old verities" (Faulkner), "the Permanent Things" (T.S. Eliot, Russell Kirk), river-beds, building blocks, originating organs, energy nodes—archetypes are the stuff that dreams, the soul, and human life are made of.

Archetypal psychology was created by James Hillman. The classic or founding text is *Revisioning Psychology*, published in 1975 and nominated for a Pulitzer.[3] Hillman has since published dozens of works—*The Thought of the Heart and the Soul of the World*, *The Soul's Code*, *A Terrible Love of War*, etc., amassed multiple honors, gathered assiduous readers, imaginative followers and talented co-workers, though he has never sanctioned nor formed the officialdom or infrastructure of a "school." Already in 1970 he had departed from the classical Jungian model of "analytical psychology," in which he was trained, to insist that: "The archetype is the most ontologically fundamental of all Jung's psychological concepts, with the advantage of precision and yet by definition partly indefinable and open. Psychic life rests upon these organs . . . Placing archetypal prior to analytical gives the psyche a chance to move out of the consulting room. It gives an archetypal perspective to the consulting room itself. After all, analysis too is an enactment of an archetypal fantasy."[4] By re-founding psychology as a discipline of reflection on archetypes; by adding his own emphasis on imagination—"the poetic basis of mind" and rhetoric—Jung said that "the archetypes speak high rhetoric, even bombast;" by enlarging the scope of psychological practice, so that it extends beyond the consulting room to the analysis of culture, and by subordinating analysis to the archetypes so that different sorts of therapies might be distinguished by the different archetypes that they enact, Hillman legitimizes the approach taken here as it shuttles between imaginative, rhetorical reflection on an archetype, and the analysis of culture and psychotherapy. The desire is to evoke the archetype, to provide a Roman Catholic tonic to our cultural blight while also bringing the treasures of the Catholic Tradition to the practice of analysis and counseling.

The primary method of archetypal psychology is amplification. Hillman writes: "Amplification includes statements of facts and statements of essences. It is empirical and scientific in being open to all sorts of evidence. It is objective in that it does not restrict meaning to a system of private conventions set up by one school of thought. And it is phenomenological as it allows the phenomenon under scrutiny to have its full say. And because amplification comprehends an event from many sides, it prevents the building of compartments between intellect and other aspects of the psyche, between logic and psychology, which would sever a rational investigation . . . from the life of psychological reality."[5] Put simply, to know the soul of any phenomena or person, one must know the stories. And I would add, one must love to hear them retold, like the child, perhaps, who will lead us to the Kingdom and who loves to hear those stories again and again. To adduce the stories and the scholarship, the history and myths, the imagery, the philosophy, the lore and legends associated with any reality—doing so in a style that leisurely circumambulates, reverently evokes and lyrically describes, relying on the wisdom and longings of the imagination, rather than proceeding in syllogistic, linear fashion through premise and conclusion, definition and logic—represents what may prove a very quixotic attempt to re-soul, to re-mythologize, to re-enchant, to re-sacramentalize the world, to recover the divine refulgences of history, the luminosities of daily life. But it is my object here. The legendary Catholic writer, "Christendom's Troubadour," as he has been styled,[6] Frederick D. Wilhelmsen, once wrote: "So far as I can see, conservatism makes no sense except when seen as the party of enchantment."[7] In another place, Wilhelmsen laments that Catholics have nothing left to do in history now that we have been denuded of our exoteric civilizing mission.[8] Amplification may be the last principled, theoretical stand of the conservative Catholic, the reactionary; or, perhaps, prologue to resurgence.

Nonetheless, with this as background, as foreground, I mean archetypal psychology not as a set of principles, whether articulated by James Hillman or anyone else; nor is it to be identified with any series of books or articles on an "approved authors" list. Least of all is it an ideology of polytheism, as in David Miller and the "Syracuse" school;[9] nor soul, as in Thomas Moore[10] and sundry others; nor archetypal psychology as a Jungian or post-Jungian approach (Andrew Samuels[11] and many of Hillman's followers). Instead, I mean archetypal psychology as a craft, a way of doing psychology. Praxis is decisive here. To be "psychological" means to be intensely intellectual, thoroughly philosophical, impressionistic, intuitive, improvisational, imaginative, grandly imaginative. It means to be experiential, attentive to particulars and pathology, the shadow, the quirk, the eccentricity or slip, the scent or taste, and the aesthetics that have remained invisible—glimpsed, if glimpsed at all, through a glass darkly. "Invisible connections are strongest," said Heraclitus. It means being steeped in history and tradition, in thrall to the beauty and complexity of the arts, of the image, in awe and fascinated by those sweeping, ubiquitous patterns that echo hauntingly and reverberate through history, like signs and miracles, like the beating of an angel's wings or the footsteps of the gods. It means to be reverent before ancient rite and ritual; irreverent in the face of cant, hypocrisy, rigid moralism, the inflexibilities of the "literalist" or "Philistine,"[12] in all of us. It means to be rhetorical in speech and prose and poetic in vision. It means to base one's vocation and identity, for in archetypal psychology vocation is identity, the work is all, in a poetic basis of mind. Is this book, paper, or practice archetypal psychology? To answer this exists not in its roots, whether in Jung or Corbin or Hillman or anyone else. The answer lies in the fruits. Does it bear the traits that I have listed, or not? If it does, it is archetypal psychology. If not, then no.

I would add that archetypal psychology is a Western psychology. As a craft, not an ideology, it is practiced best by those who are at home in the broad lineaments of the West, of two thousand years of Christianity, in Christendom, in the Judeo-Christian tradition, in the Roman Catholic Church and in Classical Culture. It is practiced best as a grateful—may I say pious, in the Roman sense?—inheritor of the proud and treasured legacy of Romanitas:

> Vergil constitutes a supreme embodiment of the optimism of his age. In him we may perceive the scope and character of those aspirations to fulfillment which were stirring in the contemporary world and which had come to a focus in the program of the Caesars. But this, in itself, by no means exhausts the significance of his work. For, while revealing the substance of the Augustan hope, Vergil at the same time disclosed its essential basis, relating it to a vast background of human history and giving it, indeed, a cosmic setting. Viewed in the light of his imagination, the Pax Augusta, emerged as the culmination of effort extending from the dawn of culture on the shores of the Mediterranean—the effort to erect a stable and enduring civilization upon the ruins of the discredited and discarded systems of the past. As thus envisaged, it constituted not merely a decisive stage in the life of the Roman people, but a significant point of departure in the evolution of mankind. It marked, indeed, the rededication of the imperial city to her secular task, the realization of those ideals of human emancipation toward which the thought and aspiration of antiquity had pointed hitherto in vain. From this standpoint,

the institution of the principate represented the final triumph of creative politics. For, in solving its own problem, Rome had also solved the problem of the classical commonwealth.[13]

And *Humanitas*:

> *Humanitas*—this was for Cicero the goal of man's moral and in-tellectual striving. *Humanissime*—the title of honor with which learned men of the Renaissance addressed one another.[14]
>
> Humanitas sustained the "Renaissance dream," of a faction-less universal order "reminiscent of Virgil and the *Pax Romana*, but also reminiscent of the unified Christendom of the Middle Ages, which, during the Renaissance, was manifested as a se-ries of visions of national empire. Just as Petrarch had projected a revival of the Roman hegemony, so Camoens saw Portugal as reconstructing European unity, and Ronsard and Spenser cast France and England in similar roles. The mantle of Rome passed from nation to nation."[15]

This vision influenced several of the founders of the European Union, such as Konrad Adenauer, Alcide Gaspari, and, especially, the Catholic neo-Thomist, Robert Schuman.[16]

Romanitas and *Humanitas* are akin to what Alfred Adler meant by *gemeinschaftsgefühl*: enlightened citizenship in the Republic of the Mind and Letters, an Invisible College, a Universal Church and Civi-lization, a community in the Augustinian sense of sharing "common loyalties and loves."

This last is arguable; would be rejected, in fact, by most, including perhaps Hillman himself, who practice archetypal psychology. But the argument is won or lost not in debate but in practice of the craft and its effects: for the reader, the patient, the audience, does it move the soul into connection with and contemplation of the vicissitudes, the depths, the genius, the active intelligence—*agens intellectus*, in the old language—of its variegated life?

Even more contentious would be my final point. I would argue that archetypal psychology is practiced best by those with what might be called a "reactionary" temperament—"reactionary" as defined by the poet Allen Tate: "Reaction is the most radical of programs; it aims at cutting away the overgrowth and getting back to the roots."[17] The best description of what "reactionary" means in this context comes from the beautiful prose of Nicolas Gomez Davila in his essay, "The Authentic Reactionary": "The reactionary does not extol what the next dawn must bring, nor is he terrified by the last shadows of the night. His dwelling rises up in that luminous space where the essential accosts him with its immortal presence. The reactionary escapes the slavery of history because he pursues in the human wilderness the trace of divine footsteps. Man and his deeds are, for the reactionary, a servile and mortal flesh that breathes gusts from the mountains . . . The reactionary is not a nostalgic dreamer of a canceled past, but rather a hunter of sacred shades upon the eternal hills."[18]

The reactionary cuts to the chase; goes to the roots. The reactionary psychologist must go to the root of his own reaction. The roots of reaction lie in revulsion, shock, disbelief, indignation. Reaction is the lion's roar. It is the thought of the heart in James Hillman's terms: " . . . the heart within the lion. The desert is not in Egypt; it is anywhere once we desert the heart. The Saints are not dead; they live in the leonine passions of the soul . . . the desert beast is our guardian in the desert of modern bureaucracy, ugly urbanism, academic trivialities, professional official soullessness, the desert of our ignoble condition."[19] The lion roars at the desert. What incites the revulsion is whatever is ignoble: the numbness to beauty, the indifference to ideals, the fetid spread of feckless self-indulgence, the apotheosis of vulgarity that characterizes so much of early twenty-first century life. The revulsion recoils from what is in essence sacrilege, from the breaking of our collective oath to preserve the fragile inheritance of what we have received. We are all oath-bound men, as Yeats says in "The Tower." The taproot of reaction lies in the denial of the debt that is owed to the Creator, to the Saints and Heroes, the Fathers and Mothers whose footsteps have preceded us, to the incomprehensible gratuity of creation. The taproot of reaction lies ultimately in a sacramental view of the world, a belief that God is present in all things. As Frederick D. Wilhelmsen stirringly proclaims:

> The Roman Catholic conserves whatever God has given him, whatever his ancestors have bequeathed him. A profound reverence for creation informs his mind, stamps itself on all his art, is translated into the way he wrestles with nature in the struggle for survival, colours his relationship with society and with the state . . . He knows the meaning of contingency, and he treads gently upon being, lest he shatter that most absolute of Gifts. He does not tinker with existence. He rather celebrates reality.[20]

The savage reaction of the reactionary—not Yeats rough beast but Hillman's lion—can only be soothed by the music of the spheres, by reversion to first principles; by the return to sources, by recollection and recovery; by reconnecting now to then, here to there, surface to depth in such a manner as to allow time to reverberate with the mysterious resonances of eternity and the present to re-present the splendor and grandeur of the past.

What does the reactionary want? As Allen Tate said of Yeats, he wants only what all men want: " . . . a world larger than himself to live in; for the modern world as he saw it was, in human terms, too small for the human spirit, though quantitatively large if looked at with the scientist."[21]

This larger life occurs with the gift of the Catholic faith. This larger life is something that can be fostered by the practice of depth psychology. A lifetime of reading Hillman, Freud, Jung, and Adler and listening hour after hour to the human soul pour out its sorrows and hopes, is sustaining. It extends the horizon; it enlarges magnitude and scope. The essential insight of depth psychology is the discovery that we all lead representative lives. Call it archetype, as I would, or heavenly sign, with Dante, or classical myth with Frazer, Freud and Jung, Campbell or Hillman, or character type or inborn temperament; call it nature or essence, call it historical cycle, national character, cultural identity or family name, it is the destiny of man through rite or ritual, education or experience, to discover what in truth he is or else drift forever as the shipwrecked *isolato*, the Ishmael "with damp, drizzly November in his soul" that the great existentialists believed us to be. The dignity of man, and his redeeming glory, when grace uplifts him, is to receive this legacy with utmost gratitude, to redeem it of its errors and evils, and, humbly, to ennoble it with the efforts of a lifetime. What is the definition of the good life, then? Stewardship, sacrifice, service. *"Ich Dien,"* the Black Prince's motto that he took from Blind King John of Bohemia, one of the great chivalric heroes.

What follows is an effort at what contemporary theorists call "epistemological consistency." For the existentialists this goal is known as "authenticity." In archetypal psychology, it is individuation as eccentricity. From my perspective, this state, as elusive as it is given the ineluctable thrust of time, consists of the "integration" for which the Christian Humanist strives.

The description is, first, of the practice of a Christian Humanist, a Catholic archetypal psychologist. Second, how does my counseling practice reflect the more encompassing and enduring themes of my daily life? Third, how does my prior writing make sense to me now in terms of a gradually crystallizing focus?

Jupiter / Strategos

To live is to maneuver.

—Whittaker Chambers

First, what is the nature of the practice?

Hilaire Belloc, the great Catholic writer, poet, and historian, once spoke of the soul of the spirit of Christendom, as its "reasonableness and chivalry." That's what I aim at: "reasonableness and chivalry," *a worldly wisdom that is a force for good*. I hope my patients become "reasonable," that is, wise in the ways of the world, that they develop a kind of worldly wisdom, about themselves, their illnesses and afflictions, about others, about the world we share, which inevitably tempers pride, kindles some gentleness and kindness with a sense that "we're all in this together." As the old saw says, "Be kind to everyone you meet, each is fighting a great battle." Also I hope they become chivalric, a "force for good" in their own life. In this world we share with others, I encourage them to speak up, speak out, stand up and maybe stand out as an example—for even in suffering, as Viktor Frankl put it, one can be exemplary, a beacon and comfort to others who too must one day walk that path.

"Reasonableness and chivalry" align with Adler's description of the aim of psychotherapy:

> The patient must be guided away from himself, toward productivity for others; he must be educated toward social interest; he must be led from his seclusion from the world, back to existence (*zurück in das Dasein*); he must be brought to the only correct insight, that he is as important for the community as anyone else; he must get to feel at home on this earth.[22]

In his clinical approach Adler epitomized worldliness. Therapy, said Adler, "requires trained sagacity and ingenuity, a jovial attitude . . . blessed with cheerfulness and good humor . . . also extreme patience and forbearance." A worldly wisdom that is a force for good is Adler's social interest, the other side of which is, as he says, courage. It is *gemeinschaftsgefuhl*. It is citizenship, a worldly cosmopolitan citizenship of the world. It is Athens, Rome, Paris, London, Vienna—Sicily, perhaps, at the court of the Norman King Roger II.

When Adler calls for a "jovial" attitude on the part of the therapist, he invokes the Roman Eagles. Adler's name means eagle. Archetypal psychology might set "reasonableness and chivalry" against an archetypal background of Jove or Jupiter, of *civus Romanus sum*, of Citizen of the Republic, the Roman Caesars, Napoleon, the Norman and Plantagenet Kings, Dante's *de Monarchia*, St. Thomas's *On Kingship, To the King of Cyprus*, or John Fortescue's political theory, a Roman psychology. It is the psychology of the crown, of the head as crown of the body. "To Julius Caesar . . . the Roman people had during his lifetime awarded 'a crown with rays' . . . He allowed himself to be represented with 'radiate head,' as did his successors. The Emperor Gallienus to make his head shine not only wore rays in public but sprinkled gold filings upon his hair. To the emperor a little later, a panegyrist speaks of 'that light surrounding your divine head in a bright circle.' It is in harmony with the belief that radiance about the head was an expression of the divine power . . . Here too perhaps is the explanation of the custom of painting with red lead the face of Jupiter's statue and also the triumphing general."[23] From the Heimskringla: "Thorir the Hound went to the spot where lay the corpse of King Olaf, and prepared it for burial . . . And when he wiped the blood from the King's face, he related afterwards, his countenance was beautiful, in that his cheeks were as ruddy as though he were asleep, and much more radiant than before when he was alive. The King's blood came on Thorir's hand and flowed between his fingers where he had been wounded before, and from that moment the wound healed so quickly . . . "[24] It is the psychology of the head as crown of the body, and reason as the crown of the head, and of judgment as the crown of reason. "The act in which the intellect knows the thing is the act of judgment, the crown of human knowledge."[25] It is a psychology whose ideas and imagery are lyrically and majestically expounded by Dante in Canto XVIII of the *Paradisio*. The themes are *recta ratio*, right reason, right action in the world. "O dulcet star! . . . Therefore I pray the Mind in which begin / Your motion and your power to attend / To where the smoke that blocks your rays arises, So that once more he may be angry with / The buying and selling in the temple / Whose walls were built by miracles and martyrs. / O soldiery of heaven on whom I gaze / Pray for all who stray from the straight path / By following bad example down on earth." The images are the Roman Eagle. "I saw the head and shoulders of an eagle / Presented in the patterned points of flame. / And the souls of chivalric warriors rising to heaven like sparks struck from a soothsayer's log. More than a thousand lights appeared to rise / From there and soar."

It is the psychology of the American Caesar, Douglas MacArthur: "He was a great thundering paradox of a man," begins William Manchester's magisterial biography. One of his generals, Robert L. Eichelberger, wrote with derision: "We have difficulty following the satellites of MacArthur, for like those of Jupiter, we cannot see the moons on account of the brilliance of the planet . . . even the gods were alleged to have their weaknesses." Manchester continues: "Such feelings were rare, and in fact Eichelberger, highly ambivalent toward his chief, was constantly torn between disillusion and encomiums to him, but it is remarkable that anyone capable of criticism remained in this Jupiter's presence."[26]

Ortega offers philosophical expression to the Jupiter archetype:

> Culture springs forth and lives, flowers and bears fruit, in a spiritual tone that is instinct with good humor—a kind of joviality. Seriousness will come later . . . But for the moment the tone is joviality. This is not a state of mind which can be regarded as in any way contemptible; remember that joviality is no less than the state of mind in which Jove usually found himself. In training ourselves to joviality we do it in imitation of Olympic Jove.[27]

> And so Plato in his last works is pleased again and again to play with two words which in Greek sound almost alike—"paideia," culture, and "paidia," child's play, jest, joviality . . . So one is invited to a hard game, for man is in the game where it is most rigorous. This jovial intellectual rigor is theory, and as I said, philosophy, a poor little thing, is no more than theory.[28]

Jupiter is the archetype that quickens Nietzsche's *gaya scienza,* to which Adler was probably alluding with his mention of joviality. Nietzsche's is, as Bachelard writes: "an 'ascensional psyche' whose totemic animal is the bird: 'and if this is my alpha and omega, that all is heavy and grave should become light: all that is body, dancer; all that is spirit, bird . . . ' This bird is predatory . . . Nietzschean flight is characterized by impetuosity and aggressiveness: 'I flew, quivering, an arrow, through sun drunken delight . . . ' It seems the eagle claws the sky: 'My eagle is awake and honors the sun as I do. With eagle talons he grasps for the new light.' Air, like all other elements, needs it warrior . . . The imagination is destined to be aggressive."[29] With the *gaya scienza* Nietzsche thought to re-Latinize the North, as happened when the French King, Charles VIII, took his armies South. Belloc writes:

> For to the North of the Alps all society reeked of the common-place and of routine . . . All that had been the sap of the thir-teenth century was dried up in the fifteenth . . . But on the South of the mountains, with a suddenness that was partly caused and partly symbolized by their terrible escarpment, it was spring. Italy, that had missed the renewal of the early Middle Ages, now, when all Europe was old, discovered her own fountains again, and dug for them in her own soil . . . The old Middle Ages of the north were in doubt and without a guide when they came in this march upon the statuary and the arches and preached a pagan gospel of splendour. Their conversion was immediate, and the soldiers found that France in Italy was an Antaeus: re-Latinized, and therefore on the high way to new vigor.[30]

Or has happened centuries before when the Northmen, sea-roving pirates out of pagan Scandinavia, became the Normans who eventu-ally were known throughout Europe as "the Sword of the Papacy." Nietzsche's blonde barbarian was not a Viking, not a Nordic super-man; or, perhaps, he was: a Romanized Viking, a Norman Lord, such as Robert Guiscard, the "other" Conqueror, not of England but of Sicily. Nietzsche wrote part of the *Gaya Scienza* in Sicily. Nietzsche always looked South for renewal, to Italy and Sicily. "O for a beaker of the warm south," said Keats. But it was the Latin world, Rome, Jove, Jupiter, not Greece. Yes, Nietzsche loved the Greeks, but he loved them as the Roman does, through right of conquest, so that he might "give style to character," may keep the mask jovial and bright when it otherwise might become too heavy. But gravitas is still the thing, the "whole slab of antiquity, perhaps even the decisive piece, the piece of granite." In a note called "Our faith that Europe will become more virile," Nietzsche says about Napoleon, "Napoleon, who considered modern ideas and civilization itself almost as a personal enemy, proved himself through this enmity as one of the greatest continuators of the Renaissance; he brought back again a whole slab of antiquity, perhaps even the decisive piece, the piece of granite."[31] Nietzsche's bird, his eagle, perhaps his swan, "the feathered glory," was Jove, the Jove of Yeats' poem "Leda and the Swan": "So mastered by the brute blood of the air, / Did she put on his knowledge with his power / Before the indifferent beak could let her drop?" In all of history does a more Nietzschean figure step forth, than the golden-voiced Norman minstrel-knight Taillefer who, when the armies were drawn up at Hastings, Saxon facing Norman, broke from the line and began to chant *The Song of Roland* until the other Knights joined in, and then tossing his sword twice into the air and catching it, led the charge, only to be cut down, the first Norman to die in England. Belloc saw the Norman victory as the re-Latinization of England, the restoration of its union with Romanitas.

The archetype's historical expression is Scipio Africanus about whom the eminent, authoritative military historian B.H. Liddell Hart wrote a book entitled *Scipio Africanus: Greater than Napoleon*. Scipio fostered the belief that he was the son of Jupiter:

> It is recorded that the mother of Scipio Africanus, the elder, had the same experience as Olympias, Philip the Great's wife and Alexander the Great's mother . . . his mother had long been believed sterile and that Publius Scipio, her husband, had despaired of having children. Then, while her husband was away and she was sleeping on her own, a huge snake was seen beside her, in her room and in her bed; when those who saw this snake shouted out in terror, it vanished and could not be found . . .

Not long after . . . the woman began to show all signs of being pregnant; in the tenth month, she gave birth to this Publius
Africanus, the man who defeated Hannibal . . . But it is much
more because of his achievements than because of that prodigy
that he . . . is thought to be a man of godlike quality. It is worth
adding that the same authorities also record that this same Africanus used to go on to the Capitol in the dead of night, before
dawn had appeared, and have the shrine of Jupiter opened for
him; he would remain there for a long time, as though he were
consulting with Jupiter about the state of the Republic. The
caretakers of the temple were often astonished that the temple
dogs never barked . . . [32]

In Liddel Hart's estimation, Scipio's preeminence as Captain resides in his precedence "as general, as man, and as statesman." As
general: "Finally, let us point out that while Alexander had the military foundations laid by Phillip to build on, while Hannibal built on
Hamilcar, Caesar on Marius, Napoleon on Carnot—Scipio had to re-
build on disaster." As man, " . . . he may, with some justice, be termed
the founder of Roman civilization." And, "By any moral test Scipio
is unique among the greater captains, possessing a greatness and pu-
rity of soul which we might anticipate, not necessarily find, among
the leaders of philosophy or religion, but hardly among the world's
supreme men, but he was no narrow patriot, instead a true world
statesman." The touchstone of his genius was as *strategos*, strategist.
"In the future, even more economic and political forces, which are
inseparable in strategy. Because Scipio more than any other great
captain understood and combined these forces in his strategy . . . the
study of his life is peculiarly apposite today."[33]

In the Roman, Latin tradition *recta ratio* has long been associated
with Jupiter.[34] From a Dantean point of view right reason is the right

reason of Thomistic epistemology where imagination, the image, the phantasm, is the indispensable and never-effaced foundation of our knowledge, the integral medium through which and by which every act of intellection occurs:

> Metaphysical insights are illuminated within phantasm-symbol constructs dependent on historical, psychological, and social circumstances. The metaphysical habitus, once born in a man, can be nourished and deepened only by a continuing and never-ending engagement in the symbolic order . . . St. Thomas often insists that anyone seeking to know any nature must erect a symbol of it through which he will "read" its meaning . . . the approach to being through phantasms is consubstantial with humanity because man understands nothing without them. [35]

In Moby Dick it is Bulkington who is Melville's image of right reason and about whom Charles Olsen writes:

> "Right reason" is the other way to God. It is the way of man's sanity, the pure forging of his intelligence in the smithy of life . . .
> Bulkington is the man who corresponds to "right reason." Melville describes him once early in the book when he enters the Spouter Inn. "Six feet in height, with noble shoulders, and a chest like a coffer dam." In the deep shadows of his eyes "floated some reminiscences that did not seem to give him much joy."
> The rest of the Pequod's voyage Bulkington remains a "sleeping partner" to the action. He is the secret member of the crew, below deck always, like the music under the earth in Antony and Cleopatra, strange. He is the crew's heart, the sign of their paternity, the human thing. And the human thing alone can reach their apotheosis.[36]

The right reason of Bulkington contrasts with the archetypal imagination of Pip, who saw "God's foot upon the treadle of the loom and
spoke it." The destiny of Ishmael is to analogically ground the right
reason of Bulkington in the archetypal imagination of Pip. With the
sinking of the Pequod, Ishmael comes in time to see God's foot upon
the loom but then to re-emerge, baptized as it were, reborn into community, the fullness of human experience and tragedy, into "worldly
wisdom as a force for good," as it were. In the magnificent novel,
Melville offers us a glimpse of Ishmael's life, post sinking of the ship,
after his night sea journey: we encounter him aboard a ship in the
company of "Spanish Dons," emblems themselves of a "worldly wisdom that is a force for good."

The chivalry here is not the chivalry of Apollo or Mars, not the
chivalry of the young beau. Nor is it the "wise old man." It is the
chivalry of Jupiter, of Barbarossa on crusade dying in the saddle at
67, of Grizzlebeard in Belloc, of the seasoned warrior, the King in the
saddle, of the beau sire, of William the Conqueror, on his knees in
prayer or at Hastings:

> The exhaustion suffered by the opposing thousands was greater
> upon the side of the attack . . . The strain and confusion was
> such that in the latter part of the action, perhaps in the mid-
> afternoon and not long before the close, the cry ran along the line
> of the invaders that William himself had fallen, and there seems
> to be some short period of lull during which the cohesion of the
> offensive was in peril. It might have broken and decided the day
> . . . In that lull the Duke by his personal action rallied the line.
> Horses had been killed under him; he rode on a fresh mount up
> and down before them, having lifted his helm from his head so
> that his face could be seen, and so inspired the final and desper-
> ate effort which was to be made.[37]

It is the chivalry of William Marshall, Earl and Regent of England, on his deathbed:

> The next day, William the Younger, kneeling, begged his father, for the love of Christ to eat something: "We are certain it will do you good." "Then for that," he acquiesced, "I shall eat as much as I can." Out of kindness. He sat up, supported by a knight. When the cloth was laid, he summoned John d'Erley. "Do you see what I see?" "My lord, I do not know what that might be." "By my soul, I see two men in white; one is beside me on the right, the other on the left; nowhere have I seen men so fine." "My lord, thus there comes to you a company that will lead you in the true way." The Earl began repeating: "Blessed be the Lord our God, who hitherto has granted me His grace." As for John d'Erley, he never forgave himself for not asking who these two persons were, so dazzling in their whiteness. Angels? Saints? Venerable ancestors returning to earth? Whatever they were, their presence proved that the gates of the other world were opening. These harbingers came to greet the earl, to provide him an escort. The sign was clear: he was soon to pass on.[38]

It is the chivalry of the father, the spiritual father. In his hauntingly beautiful essay "Churchill's Funeral," John Lukacs, perhaps the preeminent historian of the last half of the twentieth century, a Hungarian, who came of age in war torn Europe:

> I wrote "us" because, for the first and only time, I felt that I can write this honestly: not an Englishman, my grief was different from theirs, but at this moment—this very individual moment, since there is, curiously, not a speck of crowd psychic reaction in this turning around—we are all one . . . It is not perhaps the scene which is unforgettable: it is the occasion. Farewell

Churchill. Farewell British Empire. Farewell, spiritual father. Of many. Including myself.[39]

It is the chivalry of the grandfather, of the royal touch, the rite by which the touch of the King heals the commoner:

> In a news film I once saw a flick of a Churchill gesture that I cannot forget. He is coming through the ruins of an East London street after one of the bombardments. There are people, including a woman, with blowing hair, like the spirit of a proletarian Boadicea, running up to him from the ruins, gathering around him as he marches through the rubble in his tall hat and coat and cane, smoking with his incomparable chewing smile. As one of them runs up, he pats her on the back with his left arm, with a There, there! There, there! Gesture. It is an amiable, patronizing, and nonchalant everyday gesture. For a moment one senses that feeling of utter trust and confidence which only certain grandfathers can give.[40]

As with every archetype, Jupiter casts a shadow. He possesses a darker side. In a human world shot through with imperfection, right reason and chivalry are never pure. Worldliness becomes world weary, cynical. "After me, the deluge," said Tiberius. Augustine mutates into Tiberius, who immured in his island villa in Capri, rules wisely and justly, so that Robert Kaplan considers him an icon of his warrior politics,[41] but amid undeserving favorites, such as Sejanus, and rumors, justified or not, of perversity. The court breeds cronyism and corruption. The King becomes a despot engulfed by depravity. The royal line decays. Augustus, Tiberius, Claudius, then Caligula. Chivalry, a force for good, unleashes the dogs of war that, too far away from central command, become jackals, the day of the jackal, bent on assassination and slaughter. Irregulars torture, maim, plunder, loot, deface the bodies of the dead. Awash with sweat and blood and battle lust, Norman knights slash and disfigure the body of the Saxon King Harold as he takes the swan's road. But William halts them and bids the body borne away with dignity and honor. Or else, a force for good deteriorates into conniving manipulation, behind the scenes string pulling for the sheer pleasure of it. Jupiter as Puppeteer, Jesuit, or Godfather as in the cover image and logo of Puzo's novel and the movie.

As Heidegger and Dostoevsky, say, or Sartre and Kafka, are to existentialism or as the alchemists to Jung, or as the neo-Platonists and Corbin are to Hillman, so St. Thomas and Dante are to this approach. St. Thomas is the foundation, the Saint, the Doctor of the Church, the sublime philosopher, the poet and the alchemist, the Norman and the Lombard, and also the worldly St. Thomas of the Hohenstaufen Renaissance. "In the bosom of Western Christendom of the second millennium a world view was already preparing, independently, which was much akin to the Aristotelian world view, an element that quickly made common cause with the other. This element arising of its own accord in Western Christendom has been called the 'Hohenstaufen spirit.'" The whole era of the Hohenstaufens, it has been said, must be understood as a rebellion against the old Augustinian-Cluniac doctrine of the inferiority of the natural world—that is, against contempt for the world. "The whole of the courtly chivalric culture restores its due to the world and the here-and-now." The same author states that Thomas Aquinas' Aristotelian cosmology was literally "the subsequent philosophical justification for the attitude which Hohenstaufen poetry and the Hohenstaufen spirit had long since assumed . . . Thomas likewise was closely connected with Hohenstaufen circles through his father and brother, who were

among the courtiers of Frederick II."[42] Dante is the poet of Christian
chivalry, of what the great German poet and novelist Reinhold Schneider calls the "body of knights" and about which Hans urs von
Balthasar has written: "The West is born of the spirit of chivalry . . .
Only the absolute kernel of the West will understand this call, viz
the body of knights that has always prevailed in the most sublime
motifs and forms of its literature, in Dante, in Comoes, in Calderon
and Corneille, in the best of Shakespeare and in the few peaks of German literature that attain this sphere. (Quoting Schneider): 'It is here
that the great motifs of Western literature shine out. All of them are
basically an inheritance from the crusaders: chivalry and a mighty
yearning for great breadths, for the totality of the world, for eternal
life and eternal honor.'"[43]

As models of "reasonableness and chivalry," a worldly wisdom
that is a force for good, I would propose the great Pope Julius II.

> Whatever may have been the private morals of Julius II, in all
> essential respects he was the savior of the papacy. His familiarity
> with the course of events since the pontificate of his uncle Sixtus
> had given him profound insight into the grounds and conditions
> of papal authority. On these he founded his own policy, and de-
> voted to it the whole force and passion of his unshaken soul. He
> ascended the steps of St. Peter's chair without simony and amid
> general applause, and with him ceased, at all events, the undis-
> guised traffic in the highest offices of the Church . . . What Julius
> elsewhere acquired, either on the field of battle or by diplomatic
> means, he proudly bestowed on the Church, not on his family . . .
> He made himself heir of the cardinals, and, indeed, of all the cler-
> gy who died in Rome, and this by the most despotic means, but
> he murdered or poisoned none of them. That he should himself
> lead his forces into battle was for him an unavoidable necessity,

and certainly did nothing but good . . . Be this as it may, the powerful, original nature, which could swallow no anger and conceal no genuine good will, made on the whole the impression most desirable in his situation—that of the *pontifice terribile*.[44]

Also Eleanor of Aquitaine in her own court of Poitiers:

At the culmination of the queen's significant remarks, the court adjourns to the pleasance for a breath of air. Lent is over . . . The queen moves among her guests—bishops and clerks, conteurs and troubadours, the vassals of great fiefs, the princesses of France, the Poitevin ladies of the courts of love, her daughters, nieces, cousins, her fideles . . . They whisper of conspiracies and counter conspiracies in Paris, even in Poitiers. Here is the very center of rumor and surmise, and pitchers with big ears gather information to distill elsewhere.[45]

Or, perhaps, in Vienna, Adler's friend:

"Anna Sacher was one of my friends," Adler told the writer proudly; "though not until later in my life. She had a great deal of character and most of it was good."

It was not for nothing that Anna Sacher was the only woman who ever had a cake, a race horse, and a street named after her. She ruled a choice circle of Vienna aristocracy with a well-garlanded rod of iron. She was not only a first class cook and the intelligent organizer of the best restaurant in Vienna; she was the counselor, and the well-trusted counselor, of kings.[46]

Worldly, yes, but the spiritual dimension is not bypassed. The goal is the archetypal one, so well described by Hillman, in multiple papers, of a spirit and soul conjunction. Worldly virtue must reflect the theological virtues of faith, as in whatever else is true, the fact that a human person exists is an extraordinary thing, a gratuitous gift—true and good and worth exploring; hope, as in whatever dark night approaches therapist and patient, like two men lost at sea, must pull together to get by, to make sense and make the best of whatever faces them, whatever must be endured; and charity, as in speaking and listening and in being kind to one's self, with tenderness and honesty, and, as best one can, to others, is part of finding the long road back and the best road forward. Worldly virtue must be annealed in theological virtue. Hero as Saint, Saint as Hero, as Ideal.

Robert Louis Stevenson once valuably wrote: "It is the history of kindnesses that alone makes this world tolerable. If it were not for that, for the effect of kind words, kind looks, kind letters, multiplying, spreading, making one happy through another and bringing forth benefits, some fifty, some a thousand fold, I should be tempted to think our life a practical jest in the worst possible spirit."[47] Kindness is the virtue that binds Saint to Hero.

An image comes to mind from the movie, *El Cid*. The Cid encounters a leper at a well and shares his drink with him. The leper drinks greedily, returns the cup, then says: "Thank you, my Cid." With surprise the Cid, who is in exile and shabbily dressed, responds: "How do you know me?" "Who else," replies the leper, "in all of Spain could humble a King but would share his cup with a leper?" "Who are you?" asks the Cid. "My name" says the leper, "is Lazarus."

Spirituality is not ethereal, not unworldly, not disembodied, puritanical, nor limply pious. About St. Francis and St. Thomas, two of our most beloved Saints, Chesterton writes: "Perhaps it would be too paradoxical to say that these two saints saved us from Spirituality; a dreadful doom . . . But it is to say the truth in its simplest form; that they both reaffirmed the Incarnation by bringing God back to earth."[48] Once upon being asked by an usher to kneel when he was standing (as is the French fashion), Belloc shot back "Go to Hell," to which the usher responded: "Sorry Sir, I did not know that you were Catholic."

St. Thomas was a worldly philosopher, in attitude and articulation. Chesterton commends him: "(St. Thomas) . . . came out of a world where he might have enjoyed leisure, and he remained one of those men whose labor has something of the placidity of leisure . . . He had something indefinable about him, which marks those who work when they need not work. For he was by birth a gentleman of a great house, and such repose can remain as a habit, when it is no longer a motive. But in him it was expressed only in its most amiable elements; for instance, there was possibly something of it in his effortless courtesy and patience."[49] In articulation St. Thomas affirmed the value of creation. "They hold a plainly false opinion who say that in regard to the truth of religion it does not matter what a man thinks about the Creation so long as he has the correct opinion concerning God. An error concerning the Creation ends as false thinking about God." As well, he held that "The soul united with the body is more like God than the soul separated from the body because it possesses its nature in more complete fashion." St. Thomas maintained that there was sex in Paradise, that sensuality was good, anger was good, sexuality was good, so much so that he calls "unsensuality" a moral defect.

Dante, too, was worldly—sensual as befits a poet, but also civic-minded. *Civus Romanus sum.* "Dante abandons mediaeval asceticism to revert to the lay ideal, the classical ideal of the good citizen living by the inspired Roman laws. To be sure, he glorifies St. Francis' marriage to Poverty and St. Dominic's marriage to Faith, and he insists that the Franciscans remain poor friars and the Dominicans faithful preachers. But those who are of the world should not refuse to act: they have to maintain justice in the world. Each man has a duty to which he must be faithful."[50] Dante is also an archetypal psychologist whose view of the gods is singularly favorable. For Dante, "The pagan deities which the Romans invoked were natural forces providentially designed for the moral guidance of the ancient world. This rehabilitation of the religious beliefs of the Romans enables Dante to reverse the Christian view of their entire civilization. Inspired by God through the intermediary of the Muses, the Roman poets could not be liars; they were vessels of truth; directed by God through the intermediary of Jupiter, the Roman state could not be guilty of murderous aggression: Roman victories were the triumph of justice . . . The Christian poet, living in what has been called the Golden Age of the Church, preaches a moral renovation which is a return to the Golden Age of Rome. Governed by their God-given emperor and fortified by the stars, the Romans were a chosen people. Like the teachings of their poets and the laws of their rulers, their moral life was a providential example for the edification of Christians."[51] Spurning indignantly Augustine's mockery of Jupiter in The City of God: "When Dante invokes the name of 'Highest Jove' in the Purgatory, after his passionate indictment of Italian corruption, he adds: 'Who wast on earth crucified for our sake.' This identification of the tutelary deity of Roman Justice with the God of the Christians is more than a verbal confusion or a rhetorical device. It is the summary of all we have said so far . . . Dante maintains that the Romans, through the Providence of God, possessed the truth of justice."[52]

As a Roman Catholic Counselor, as a man inspired and nourished by both the tradition of Catholic, Thomistic philosophy, the chivalry of Catholic heroes, the beauty of Catholic art, the sanctity of Catholic Saints, and imbued, I think, with a Dantean ethos, when I write a case study, as I often do, I always end up writing a Romance, a Saga, about the beauty and heroism of the human spirit. How could it be otherwise? *La Vita Nuova!* "And so I decided to take as the theme of my writing from then on whatever was praise."[53]

How do I work? An old French saying avers that "if you wish to learn how to jump a horse, throw your heart over the fence first, the horse will follow"—a worthy motto that I have tried to make my own, as a therapist and as a man. I do it by throwing my heart and mind into the matter at hand. I do it by being myself, by brainstorming and talking a blue streak, and listening and comforting and empathizing in a conversation whose ideas, images, plans of action, new perspectives I hope the patient finds interesting, useful, valuable, comforting, pleasing, above all truthful, because if truthful, freeing, because the Truth will set you free.

To meet the patient with a clinical approach that also "throws one's heart across the fence," is only fair, the only way to do justice to that extraordinary act of starting therapy. When a patient makes the first call, when he comes in for the first session, he throws his heart across the fence. He judges; he risks; he opens himself to unfamiliar territory; he hopes; he dreams; he faces the unknown; he displays a considerable courage. Somehow in the deepest recesses of his being he understands and stakes his claim that, as Wilhelmsen says:

> . . . there can be no true love of the other without a love of the self . . . Man's ecstatic affirmation of the other is his affirmation of his own existence, an existence which is totally thrown out toward the world in an embrace as broad as being itself. This opening of man to being, together, with this fulfilling of being by man, is the ecstasy in which history is born. It is an ecstasy defining the Catholic affirmation of being, and the Catholic order

stands to this ecstasy of love in a relation which is proportionate to Protestantism's salute to the courage to be.[54]

For a therapist to start as well by throwing his heart across the fence is to extend the traditional medical, alchemical, homeopathic and Jungian idea that like cures like. For an Adlerian it is meeting a client's nascent social interest with social interest. For hypnosis it is "matching." For an Ericksonian it is "utilizing the given." For an existentialist it is the "Thou" meeting the "I" in reciprocal response made in hospitality, mutuality and trust. Such an approach fulfils the therapeutic injunction familiar to every social worker, counselor, family therapist, psychologist, psychiatrist and analyst: the therapist must meet the client where he is.

Can I be more specific? Yes. I throw my heart across the fence in this way. I envision. In my mind's eye I see a vision of the world as it is, a noble, wonderful, magnificent place and the patient too, as he or she could be, noble, wonderful, magnificent. "Your life is a monument" as Frankl often said. Wilhelmsen writes:

> For any creature to be at all is for it to be a way of being God-like. The Thomistic understanding of being easily fructifies into a sacramental vision of the real. And each reality is itself a gift of being rather than a recipient of that gift of being because before God created that reality, it was, quite literally, simply nothing at all. For Christians Being is a gift, and our response to such a dazzling inheritance as Being is to bend the knee in thanksgiving, thus saying to God through His World: Amen.[55]

In other words, I begin as a Thomist-Dantean, with a Catholic sacramental view. I mention Frankl. Many examples of this exist in logotherapy. In *Everyday Mysteries* Emmy van Deurzen comments:

For Frankl, ideals are not something to be sneered at, for they are the very stuff of survival. When speaking to a terminally ill patient, he says, "Your life is a monument," encouraging the person to suffer with dignity. He reminds a bereft person, who has lost a sense of meaning since the death of his wife, that being bereft of his wife is a final gift he can offer her – in sparing her the grief she would have had to suffer if he had been the first to die. To those struggling to live a decent life, he gives the following categorical imperative: "Live as if you were living already for the second time and as if you had acted the first time as wrongly as you are about to act now."[56]

Like Frankl, I envision with a patient. Churchill did it for a nation:

The Oxford philosopher Isaiah Berlin remarked that Churchill "idealized" his countrymen "with such intensity that in the end they approached his ideal and began to see themselves as he saw them."[57]

I vision and I strategize. Haley introduced strategy into therapy. After his death Haley was recalled by friends: "Jay Haley, more than anyone, integrated the therapist's use of empathy with the use of clever strategy. He oriented therapists to become practical and helpful by focusing on the person's social-existential situation. In his view the therapist was not to be a wandering analytic soul companion, but rather a down to earth, relief oriented, context changing craftsman" (Braulio Montalvo). "He was a kind, true gentleman and a scholar" (Scott R. Wooley). Haley admired Erickson's genius, but also his physical endurance and strength, while regretting the "guru-fication" of Erickson as the "sage of Phoenix," the "wise old man," a sort of "Southwesternized" Jung—more *brujo* and Castaneda's Don

Juan than the Celtic Merlin. In an interview Haley remembered him: "This man was seeing patients from 7:00 in the morning until 11:00 at night and giving seminars every couple of weeks, and was always teaching . . . One of the reasons I didn't see him so often during the 1970s is that I was feeling sad about him. When I knew him, he was a physically strong man, and very articulate. He was one of the few therapists who said it was extremely important to control your physical movement, and to control your voice . . . I mean he was physically very active when I knew him." This admiration for Erickson's mental and physical strength, for his Kennedyish "vigor,"—we once expected it from Supreme Court Judges too, for example, Justice William Douglas—or the Renaissance *virtu* that characterized Pope, Prince, poet and condottiere, combing moral, physical and imaginative force, was prefigured in *Uncommon Therapy*: "A part of Erickson's confidence in his approach to patients is the sureness of his own moral posture. He had definite ideas about how people should behave, and yet at the same time he is tolerant of the various ways of living there are in this culture. His moral position is not rigid; yet he does not continually question it as many liberal intellectual therapists do." "Erickson is willing to use his physical handicaps as part of the therapeutic procedure. Often the extent of his handicap is underestimated: after his first attack of polio, when he was seventeen he made a thousand-mile canoe trip alone to build up his strength, and after his second attack, in 1952, he took one of the more difficult hikes in Arizona, walking on two canes."[58] Haley thought of therapy in terms of strategies, strength, stamina, skills, and, like the medieval Samurai or other Japanese practitioners of the "Way," looked to Zen for orientation: "I was very much influenced by Zen in terms of an ideology about life. Ultimately I realized that Zen practices and Erickson's therapy were similar in many ways."[59]

Adler's friends and biographers often comment on his physical strength, robust health, Spartan habits, swimming and hiking, fortitude and endurance. To admire such characteristics is probably universal; to regard them as defining of character is not. Such admiration typifies a Jupiterian world-view, an archetypal matrix and hierarchy of values. It is not the grace or ferocity of the athlete, or the martial warrior; it is not the restless energy of the merchant, the smoothness of the diplomat, the grave dignity of the blacksmith, or the sober mien of the judge. It is not Apollo or Mars, Mercury or Pluto. It is the invincibility of the general in the field, of the Caesar showing himself to the troops. It is courage of fortitude; the courage neither of the cavalry charge or cold steel, but of iron will. It is the courage of application, industry, endurance—what Adler, called training. It is the courage of the Samurai and Shogun, and the Legionnaire, the Foreign Legion too, the courage of the French at Dien Bien Phu. It is Roman courage. The courage of Pompeii and Caesar, Augustine and Marcus Aurelius. It is General Pershing at middle age leaving Patton in the dust in the Mexican desert:

> General P and Barker and Boyd and I went hunting antelope east of Camp. The Gen got one shot at about 400 yards. We rode part way back and got into an auto leaving horses. After a little it stuck in the mud so Gen, Barker, and I started to walk. We did four miles in 50 minutes the General setting the pace. Hardest walking ever did. Barker and I were stiff for several days.[60]

It is MacArthur in his sixties, in the South Pacific, astonishing the "doc."

> One of the aides cowering on the deck on the little vessel was Dr. Egeberg, who did not regard himself as a man of destiny and

felt the need for precautions strongly. He forgot his qualms on the shores of Humboldt Bay, however, where his professional curiosity was aroused by his patient's physical performance. Aged sixty-four, the General was by far the oldest member of the party, yet he took off on a brisk three-hour hike, leaving the others, physician noted, "panting hard." Not only wasn't he out of breath, despite the equatorial heat, he wasn't even sweating.[61]

It is FDR, who "to compensate for his withered limbs . . . lifted weights to build his upper body, which became so strong that the skinny young man with the fey affect now appeared barrel-chested and manly in photographs," . . . and, on his inauguration day . . . "wore no overcoat against the chill wind, though a similar decision by William Henry Harrison at his 1841 Inauguration had famously caused his death from pneumonia a month later. FDR was determined to wear nothing over his formal morning coat, a signal effort to seem healthy and vigorous."[62]

This is Jupiter. The physical type recurs. The general is tall, like Washington: "six foot two in stocking, weighing one hundred and seventy five pounds . . . with well developed muscles . . . wide shouldered . . . neat waisted . . . blue-gray and rather penetrating eyes." Or de Gaulle:

> . . . de Gaulle's physique helped to reinforce the impression of a huge personality. He was tall; not absurdly so—at six foot five inches—but tall enough to stand out. What made his natural height the more striking was his upright, almost stiff, military bearing and his long neck. He appeared as someone used to giving commands and seeing them obeyed.[63]

Or is remembered as very tall, though in fact, like MacArthur, like Lee, like William the Conqueror, he was less than six feet. In presence, he is imposing, impressive, massive and magnificent in physique: he possesses weight, authority, gravitas, like General Chiarelli taking command in Bagdad:

> He had turned fifty-four a few days earlier. In his middle age, he was beefy and imposing, no longer the slightly plump and easily awed officer he had once been. Along with his desert fatigues and body armor, he wore the wraparound sunglasses and high suede boots favored by tankers. In his battle garb he resembled a stiff gaited robot warrior . . . [64]

Or Robert E. Lee:

> General Lee looked very much jaded and worn, but nevertheless presented the same magnificent physique for which he has always been noted. He was neatly dressed in gray cloth, without embroidery or any insignia of rank, except the three stars worn on the turned portion of his coat-collar. His cheeks were very much bronzed by exposure, but still shone ruddy underneath it all. He is growing quite bald, and wears one of the side locks of his hair thrown across the upper portion of his forehead, which is as white and fair as a woman's. He stands fully six feet one inch in height, and weighs something over two hundred pounds, without being burdened with a pound of superfluous flesh. During the whole interview he was retired and dignified to a degree bordering on taciturnity, but was free from all exhibition of temper or mortification. His demeanor was that of a thoroughly possessed gentleman who had a very disagreeable duty to perform, but was determined to get through it as well and as soon as he could.[65]

As he ages, he "hides his paunch like a state secret," as was said of MacArthur (who did sit-ups every morning throughout his life) or de Gaulle or William the Conqueror, whose enemies whispered—but only, whispered, mind you—that the King looked like he was pregnant.

In complexion he is ruddy like Olaf, like the Conqueror or Guiscard, or Lee or Patton, who suffered severe burns on his face during the expedition in Mexico and was often described in later years as flushed, pink-cheeked or reddening. MacArthur coming East to West Point was described as "outdoorsy and ruddy." Or General Forrest, who though not born to the purple in a Roman world might very well have risen to it. "The names of many Roman grandees poignantly reveal their peasant origin. Cincinnatus and Calvus ('Curly' and 'Baldy') . . . Crassus and Macer ('Fatty' and 'Baldy') . . . the inheritors of Etruscan Kingly regalia and Greek aesthetic refinement." (The Oxford History of the Roman World.) It was said of Forrest:

> His Major, a celebrated preacher and subsequently an equally celebrated Confederate Colonel, D.C. Kelly, saw him then for the first time under fire, and thus vividly describes the wonderful change that always took place in his appearance in a fight: "His face flushed till it bore a striking resemblance to a painted Indian warrior's, and his eyes, usually so mild in their expression, blazed with the intense glare of a panther's about to spring on his prey. In fact, he looks as little like the Forrest of our mess table as the storm of December resembles the quiet of June."[66]

The image is the general in triumph, chariot elevating him above the heads of the roaring crowd, physical form massive with ritual robe and ornament, face painted red with red lead.

First to pass through the gate from the field of Mars was the entire body of the Senate, including Cicero, walking on foot, led by the consuls and the other magistrates. Then the trumpeters, sounding the fanfares. Then the carriages and litters laden with the spoils of the Spanish war . . . and wooden models of the cities Pompey had conquered and sacked, and placards with their names, and the names of all the famous men he had killed in battle. Then the massive, plodding white bulls, destined for sacrifice, with gilded horns hung with ribbons and floral gardens . . . Then trudging elephants—the heraldic symbol of the Metelli—and lumbering oxcarts bearing cages containing the wild beasts of the Spanish mountains, roaring and tearing at the bars. Then the arms and insignia of the beaten rebels, then the prisoners themselves . . . Then the crowns and tributes of the allies . . . Then the twelve lictors of the imperator, their rods and axes wreathed in laurel. And now at last, to a tumult of applause from the vast crowd, the four white horses of the imperator's chariot trotting through the gate, and there was Pompey himself, in the barrel-shaped, gem-encrusted chariot of the triumphator. He wore a gold-embroidered robe with a flowered tunic. In his right hand he held a laurel bough and in his left a scepter. There was a wreath of Delphic laurel on his head, and his handsome face and muscled body had been painted with red lead, for on this day he truly was the embodiment of Jupiter.[67]

Haley defined strategic therapy as any therapy in which the therapist makes a plan for treatment and takes responsibility for the results. As I'm an archetypal psychologist, I am a strategic therapist. I regularly deploy strategic techniques: metaphors, directives, emphasizing strengths and positives, noble ascriptions, positive connotations, frustrating changes, prescribing a relapse, accentuating differences, paradoxical intentions and I certainly strive to speak an inspirational language. The two chief ideas of strategic therapy: the family generational cycle and "incongruous hierarchy" provide productive orientation. The strategic goals of "problem solving," of making every therapeutic conversation "productive," and increased "tranquility and pleasure," are ones I endorse and belong, I think, in some sense to "reasonableness and chivalry." Diplomacy and good conversation, learning and luxury, chivalry and honor met in many a Medieval and Renaissance court. But this is not "your grandfather's" strategic therapy. On the other hand, it is your grandfather's strategic therapy. It is the Roman Catholic Archetypal Psychology of the Fathers, of the men whom I've made my fathers, the "master spirits" of the *lares* and *penates*, of the household gods, of the ancestors, of the Holy Company of Saints and heroes. It is strategic therapist against the background of St. Thomas and Dante, Adler's Viennese, cheerful, jovial, worldly, streetwise, savvy advice. It is strategic therapist against the background of Hillman's visionary archetypal psychology which is itself the psychology of background, of cultured, beautiful amplification, which is the psychology whose fundamental method of epistrophe is to return phenomena to their archetypal background and thereby discover their fructifying source.

Therapy is always a conversation, so that speaking is always a speaking-with as well as a speaking-to. Counseling is like a dance with one person leading, now another. Nevertheless, I take Jay Haley's point that therapy is always directive—even Rogerian "reflection," a conscious shaping—as irrefutably established. From an experiential point of view, Haley's assertion is merely a therapeutic acknowledgment of the "leading" nature of every question. To ask is to lead; it is to provoke an answer. A martial trumpet echoes in even the mildest question. It is the therapist's responsibility to take the lead. When a patient returns home after a first session, the first question from spouse or parent, friend or sibling, is: "What did he say?" Counseling is a person-to-person encounter, an I-Thou relationship, a collaborative relationship of mutual trust. I would define it as one of Aristotle's forms of friendship, a befriending defined by its particular boundaries. Although the counselor takes the lead, he surrenders it often; he leads, configures, shapes, asks and is asked, and answers. The ultimate responsibility for the session, nonetheless, is his.

In his fascinating *The Grand Strategy of the Byzantine Empire,* Edward Luttwak defines strategy as "the application of method and ingenuity in the use of both persuasion and force . . . strategy in all its aspects, from higher statecraft down to military tactics."[68] By clinical strategy I mean developing a plan of action that will relieve suffering—there is no virtue in needless suffering—overcome a problem, attain a goal, fulfill a dream. To be strategic means, at worst, to strive for economy; at best, elegance. A strategic plan is one that maximizes gain, while minimizing risk, loss, pain, effort. A strategic plan is to think like a consigliere: "Geraci was a reader . . . Once he finished the history of Roman warfare he'd brought with him, all he had left were the books that were already there . . . He'd already read *The Prince,* but reread it several times as a hedge against going nuts,"[69] a chess player, like a diplomat, like a political consultant. Like William the Conqueror, "the one man in Europe who understood strategy," a natural "re-framer" who falling flat on his face upon arriving on the coast of England turned the ill omen into a positive portent by saying to his comrades "See, I have taken England with both my hands." Like Cecil and Walsingham, Elizabeth's spymaster, or the Jesuits, who were more than their equals. It is to think like all those authors of the "Advice to Princes" genre: Machiavelli, Erasmus, Bolingbroke, Gracian, Castiglione. "The prince," as Hillman says, "as generous metaphor for responsible citizen and concerned member of the polis, will keep a focused mind, a mind undistracted by the multiple diversions of peace, and a psyche neither numbed nor in denial. And he will maintain this clarity not merely by meditating or praying to benefit his own 'mental health,'" but for the common good and the defense of his community. Hence the prince "ought never to let his thoughts stray from . . . war."[70] It is to think like General Jan Christian Smuts, Churchill's "personal consigliere" throughout the blood, sweat and tears ordeal of wartime Britain. Smuts, "one of his closest advisors and confidants during the war . . . He was a steadying source Churchill could turn to for sound military and political counsel . . . it was Smuts who seemed to have the greatest influence. To end one interminable late-night meeting 'Smuts sent the Prime Minister to bed, like a small boy, and he went off obediently, as though dispatched by his mother.'"[71] It is to think like Douglas MacArthur: "From some of these interchanges I got a clear picture of the connection between chess and war. He might say, 'Now if we do this, which Steve suggested, they might do this, or, if they were clever, they might do that. Now if they do this, we should answer them in one of three ways,' and he would outline the other alternative, and then he would go to the Japanese answer to the six or seven possibilities. By the time he had done this for a day or week, he would call his staff, establish the strategy which was amazingly frequently the opposite from the feeling of the majority, and which would seem always to have been right."[72]

Perhaps the idea of counselor as general is not quite as preposterous as it sounds. It accords with the ancient idea—what Hillman would call, following the philosopher Suzanne Langer, "fecund"— that Life is a Battle, which has origins in the Old Testament: *militia vita est homini* ("a soldier's service is the life of man," or so the Vulgate translates it); in the Stoics ("to live is to fight," said Seneca); in St. Paul; and stretches to Darwin ("the survival of the fittest"),

Edwin O. Wilson, and contemporary evolutionary psychology. The idea occurs as well in Blake, Nietzsche, and Norman O. Brown: From his final essay: "This world was, is, and always will be, ever-living fire. It will never be a safe place; it will never be a pastoral scene of peace and pleasure, *luxe calme et volupte*, Baudelaire's utopian image invoked by Marcuse in *Eros and Civilization*. Traces of this misleading light disfigure the last chapter of *Life Against Death*."[73] If Life is a Battle, what would be a reasonable, a "fecund" or generative way, of imagining a therapist?—trainer, coach (Bowen), life strategist, Director of Souls, a Spiritual Director, a General, a *strategos*.

Strategic derives from the Greek word, *strategos*, meaning general. In archetypal psychology, etymology is psychology, the logos of the soul at its roots.[74] Martial strains resound hauntingly but unmistakably, like the trumpets in the Patton score, in the history of therapy. Freud cast himself, the psyche, and psychoanalytic work in a martial mold. Repression is a siege mentality, the defenses siege fortresses; psychoanalytic techniques as a series of siege engines and towers. Freud saw himself as a conquistador. As an analyst, he was more like Saladin outside of Jerusalem. Jones imagined Freud as Charlemagne and pleased him by purchasing a set of "secret rings" inset with emblems of Charlemagne's Paladins which Jones shared with the analytic elect, so that they "might guard the kingdom and policy of their master." Jung's decisive individuation dream—the one that conferred upon him what the Jungian analyst Robert Grinnell termed "faith in the psyche"—brought forth the Templar, the fullness of which he missed, I think, by not linking it with St. Francis' similar experience that analogously revealed the Saint's destiny. Adler chose to live not once, but twice, as his biographer notes, at "the exact location" where European Knight turned back the janissaries of Suleiman the Magnificent. Hillman describes his writing style, which is his style of thought, as that of a General conducting a campaign. Freud as Conquistador; Jung as Templar, Alfred Adler, for his biographer, "a Columbus of the soul." Having known Hillman I can imagine him as a Civil War general, half Sherman, half Stuart, half March to the Sea, half ride around the Union army, half all Yankee business, half Rebel cavalier panache. Napoleon complexes, all? As Nietzsche said, Homer's longing to be Achilles? Perhaps. Or perhaps war besets and embattles us as a permanent part of the human condition and as a permanent part of the imagination. Hillman makes this case in the brilliant *A Terrible Love of War*. "War as the father of all," said Heraclitus. Or for Blake, "Eden is a place of mastery, of active engagement in intellectual warfare and hunting." Wilhelmsen proclaims "Catholicism is about swords." So, too with therapy: war, mastery, swords, strategy. I'm no MacArthur; but Freud was no Charlemagne either. And Jones as Roland? Jung as Ganelon—that, I get.

The metaphor of intellectual as general is not unknown in either artistic or intellectual history. From Kurosawa to John Milius, film directors—to which early family therapists were often compared—film directors have imagined themselves as generals. Kurosawa: "A movie director is like a front-line commanding officer. He needs a thorough knowledge of every branch of the service, and if he doesn't command each division, he cannot command the whole . . . I often say, although I am certainly not a militarist, that if you compare the production unit to an army, the script is the battle flag and the director is the commander of the front line. From the moment production begins to the moment it ends, there is no telling what will happen. The director must be able to respond to any situation, and he must have the leadership ability to make the whole unit go along with his responses."[75] Sam Fuller said "film is war." John Milius: "I'm a general." Francis Ford Coppola gave the name of his mentor, Roger Corman, to the general in *Apocalypse Now*. Leaders of intellectual movements sometimes follow suit. Allen Tate and Andrew Lytle, the Fugitive Agrarians, greeted each other as "General" while they collaborated in producing the Agrarian Manifesto, *I'll Take My Stand*. Friends of Frederick Engels, Marx's co-author, teased him as "the General."

> The somber Marx . . . admired Engel's power. "He can work at any hour of the day, fed or fasting; he writes and composes with incomparable fluency." Engels himself said of his own style that, as with artillery, "each article struck and burst like a shell."
>
> Such militant vocabulary was no mere play on words. Even in his most abstract writings . . . Engels made ample use of military terms and experiences, because he was by nature a soldier and warrior. . .
>
> One may regret that the "general," as his friends jokingly nicknamed him, never had a chance to prove his mettle. Yet his influence on tactics and strategy of the Russian Revolution are well known. Even his contemporary adversaries among the military experts respected his judgment.[76]

Medieval abbots sometimes called themselves generals: " . . . for the Christian combat of which St. Benedict liked to speak, and which Origen had shown we are committed to at Baptism, is not waged alone; it is waged in common and under the leadership of a chief. Therefore sometimes we read in the eulogy of an abbot, 'that in the days of this excellent general, the soldiers of Christ advanced on the royal road.'"[77] Heads of religious orders sometimes take the title of Director-General. Occasionally the armchair strategist does take the field, as did General Vo Nguyen Giap:

> In the deadly guessing game that is grand strategy, the little Vietnamese history professor with his largely self taught military

science had totally outguessed the French generals and colonels with their general-staff diplomas.[78]

Strategy, after all, is an armchair, even air–conditioned, exercise; the blood and sweat and tears come later:

> The Battle of Dien Bien Phu was lost during the brief fortnight between November 25 and December 7, 1953. It was not lost in the little valley in Viet Nam's highland jungles but in the air conditioned map room of the French commander-in-chief. Once Giap had decided to accept trial by battle at Dien Bien Phu, it remained only for 15,000 French and 50,000 Viet-Minh troops to act out the drama in pain and blood and death.[79]

The idea of strategy must not be confined to war or military operations. Strategy is a way of thinking, a paradigm, a root metaphor. Even military writers understand this:

> While strategy is more particularly concerned with the movement of armed masses, grand strategy, including those movements, embraces the motive forces which lie behind them, material and psychological . . . The grand strategist is, consequently, also a politician and diplomatist.[80]

Strategy is thinking like a chess master, yes, elegantly, economically, the most gain with the least risk, loss, pain, damage; but the elegance expresses a comprehension of the whole in an intuitive, and, often, unrecoverable, and nearly always, indescribable flash as if in animate interplay arrayed upon a screen: strategy is guesswork; strategy is to see the big picture, the forest as well as the trees; to glimpse the numberless possibilities contained therein, their interdependency, the features that are fixed and those that are flexible, what does not change, what changes, what is changeable; and possible new combinations and how each of those combinations might provoke counter responses—resistance, surrender, feint, dodge, avoidance, evasion, diversionary tactic, counter attack, oblique, double oblique, etc.—that instantaneously alter the whole. Strategy is an exercise of judgment in the moment, in the fog of war or in the free flow of conversation, the judgment that does not so much adapt the general to the particular, as does a judge, but enacts the particular in the general as the general's most elegant and successful realization, which can never be determined, of course, save by outcome. Strategic judgment is the act in which the mind synthesizes all its body of knowledge and the depth and scope of its accumulated experience to produce an elegant form—strategy—that illumines the potential, pitfalls and purpose, the causes, connections, conditions, and context of a single experience. In therapy the strategic move may be an interpretation, an "idea," a re-frame, a metaphor, a story, a directive, etc.

Although family therapy has spent the last quarter century in full retreat from its original inspiration, at its inception it spoke a directive, martial language. "Admiral" Minuchin described "joining": "The therapist is in the same boat with the family, but he must be the helmsmen . . . What qualifications must he have? What can he use to guide the craft? . . . (He) brings an idiosyncratic style of contacting, and a theoretical set. The family will need to accommodate to this package."[81] I've seen Minuchin work: a humble sailor? Hardly. More like Master and Commander. In the classic book, *The Tactics of Change*, in a chapter on therapist maneuverability, Fisch, Weakland, and Segal write: "It may seem cold and calculating to talk about ways of controlling the process of treatment, but we believe it is evident, on a little reflection, that the client is not in a position to know how his problem should be best approached . . . Accordingly, almost all therapies involve tactics for providing therapist control of the course of treatment. However, the 'managerial' aspects of therapies are often passed over . . . This is not for the arbitrary purpose of controlling *per se*. Rather, it is ethically consistent with our view that the guidance of treatment is an inherent responsibility of the therapist and it is to the patient's detriment if the therapist abdicates this responsibility."[82] Although the battle has gone against the directive, strategic approach, Minuchin still cannot resist a Samurai story to describe his teaching style, the tale of the greatest of the Japanese samurai, Musashi, who acquired his skills through training by a mysterious half-mad martial artist monk who among others dodges and deceits, locks Musashi in a library for months. Obviously, he admires the monk, while admitting sheepishly that "To those who are sensitive to hierarchy and control issues . . . this method of samurai training would be a nightmarish learning experience."[83] Does it really put Minuchin on the couch to detect an image here of therapist as Samurai Master, as Shogun? Manchester's biography of MacArthur is called American Caesar; it could just as well have been called American Shogun, because that is what he really was. Perhaps the history of family therapy would have been different (or, at least, we would not be where we are now, which, to my mind, is reverting back to not Freud—that would not be all that regrettable; then, maybe we would attract a few more conquistadors—but to Rogers, in whom not even I with eye "passionate, fantastical" can hear a haunting Pattonesque trumpet echoing) if the MRI team, and other strategic- and solutions-based therapists, had spoken less about "controlling" the session and more about strengthening a therapeutic "alliance"—consider this!— at the very heart of therapy exists a military, strategic metaphor as a description of the single therapeutic phenomenon nearly all therapists believe to be the one, central indispensable vehicle and condition for change!—in which the therapist would assume the position of the *strategos*, while, after considering the patient's input, the patient's thoughts, the patient's advice, and, then, in the absolute act of trust that any good officer knows is essential to success, entrusting to him, the mission, development of the tactics needed to complete the mission, and, to large degree, complete freedom and entitlement to adapt or alter strategy in light of the "fog of war" and fluid conditions on the ground. It is his life, his battle. The *strategos* remains "Dugout Doug," behind the lines.

The kindest comment ever made about my style in therapy came from a hard-boiled plumber who had been in and out of therapy with a dozen different therapists for a period of over twenty years. "You play hard ball," he said, "Everybody else plays softball." A one-time patient of Hillman's told me that, "It was like he kept his thumb on the artery in your neck the whole hour, taking your pulse and applying pressure." I wish someone had said that about me.

Strategic therapy is also a family therapy. From our perspective, we may think of a family as less a "unit" seen in a consulting room which must be distinguished from an "individual" or "couple" unit, and more of family itself as a way of seeing, a style of life and imagination, a very Roman and Catholic way of seeing. As Wilhelmsen writes:

> To the old Roman at his best (and at his worst) the family is knit together by blood and a common land turned over by hands that have received their patrimony from a line of ancestors stretching back to the youth of the race. The dusk falls on the back of each man as he retreats down the road of time, but as he has received from the past, so has he given to the future, and as they lived in him, so shall he live in them. And this is promised him by the

household gods, and even when he no longer believes in gods he still keeps them, for they are the badge of his service and the pledge of his immortality.[84]

Strategic therapy as a family therapy enacts a way of seeing that identifies and privileges particular themes such as loss and love, which have been my concern, loyalty and continuity (Bowen), communication and feeling (Satir), justice and entitlement (Bozormenyi Nagy), creativity, madness, and the absurd (Whitaker), power, structure, and hierarchy (Erickson, Minuchin, Haley) and narrative (Michael White).

Strategic therapy is also a problem-solving therapy which may seem to pose a conflict with a Roman Catholic therapy that exalts the mystery, dignity, and immeasurable value of the human person. The great existential Thomist philosopher Gilson offers the corrective. In *The Christian Philosophy of Thomas Aquinas* Gilson addresses Marcel's famous distinction between problem and mystery:

> It has been rightly insisted that we must distinguish whatever separates the *problem* from the *mystery*, and upon the need for the metaphysician to pass beyond the first plane to the second. But neither is to be sacrificed for the sake of the other. When philosophy abandons the problem in order to immerse itself in the mystery, it ceases to be philosophy and becomes mysticism. Whether we like it or not, the problem is the very stuff out of which philosophy is fashioned . . . If philosophizing is a kind of examining of the real, philosophy can only deal with the real to the extent it can be problematized . . . To renounce the problematizing of mysteries would be to renounce philosophizing . . . But if we must not leave the problem alone, neither ought we to leave the mystery alone either. The real danger begins where the problem is confronted by the mystery and pretends to be suffi-

cient to itself and to lay claim to an autonomy which it does not actually possess.[85]

If the only approach to the mystery of existence is by "problematizing" it, then for a therapy that claims to be philosophically based, the best approach to the mystery of human suffering must also be to "problematize" it. It does this through a clinical process that conceptualizes it as a problem that can be successfully treated without either counselor or patient forgetting or neglecting the irreducible mystery that infuses and encompasses the nature of the problem, as immanence and transcendence, and of which the problem is an individual expression.

At its best, a Roman Catholic therapy combines a medieval, Dantean, Shakespearian sense that "the air is awash with angels" while gargoyles leer, scarlet-mantled Cardinals offer up the Host, courtiers, sly and sinister, connive, masons build, merchants hawk their wares in crowded streets, philosophers dispute with all the ferocity of tournament combatants, farmers sell their crop, a troubadour warbles on the breeze, proud-eyed, grim-visaged knights keep watch, kings conduct their councils and affairs of state; that "there are more things in heaven and earth than are dreamt of in your philosophies"; with recovery and relief. Authenticity and individuation, however they might be conceived, whether with Heidegger or Jung, or their followers, are not inimical to problem-solving and client satisfaction. The goal of "successful treatment" does not cheapen the process.

Under the banners, then, of this Catholic, Roman, Norman, Thomistic, Dantean, worldly, and chivalric psychology—let us imagine it as the flag of Normandy, three Leopards on a Scandinavian cross of red and gold, or a Papal banner if your like—Haley and Hillman meet. For a strategic therapist the image of *strategos* furnishes the archetypal background of his work, its philosophical meaning, its psychological value, its poetic beauty to the degree that it attains any. Of all the great therapists, it is easiest to think of Haley, with his wit, subtlety, urbanity, learning, and unimpeachable effectiveness as an advisor to Princes, as a feared courtier at court. Perhaps such worldly judgments are not entirely out of place in developing a worldly clinical approach. R.D. Laing once dismissed most of the great American humanistic psychologists by opining that none of them would last five minutes in a Glasgow bar. Hillman is its psychologist, its learned interpreter, the creator of a dazzling Renaissance psychology, as spacious as the Augustinian palace of memoria, about which he has written so beautifully (see his *The Myth of Analysis*) in which courtier and condottiere, monk and man of the world, merchant, magi, Prince all meet. The safe house, the meeting place is Adler's and Orson Welles' (*The Third Man*) Vienna.

Under these banners strategic techniques cease to be techniques, external skills acquired; instead, once internalized, falling on temperamentally receptive and psychologically fertile grounds, they express an attitude (Adlerian), an archetype (Jupiter), an archetypal psychology (Hillman), a history, culture, and Roman Catholic faith. In this way and under this banner this therapy lays claim to authenticity, to individuation as eccentricity, to Christian humanistic integration.

Vision, strategy, inspiration, too. Following in the footsteps of the hypnotists, those who healed beneath village trees and in the corridors of Kings, strategic therapists aspire to speak an inspirational language. Strategic therapy originated with Haley's insight that Milton Erickson's defining contribution to the field of psychotherapy is that "he broadened hypnosis beyond a ritual to a special style of communication." This special style is rhetoric.

In this view, "epideictic" appears as that which shapes and cultivates the basic codes of value and belief by which a society and culture lives; it shapes the ideologies and imageries with which, and by which, the individual members of a community identify themselves; and, perhaps, most significantly, it shapes the fundamental grounds, the "deep" commitments and presuppositions that will underlie and ultimately determine decision and debate in particular, pragmatic forums.[86]

This serves as a description of Ericksonian hypnosis. A Roman Catholic archetypal counselor must not only think like MacArthur, he must speak like him too, whether upon coming ashore in the Philippines, on the deck of the battleship Missouri accepting the Japanese surrender, or before Inchon, persuading a room of skeptical fearful Pentagon brass and fellow officers, or at West Point, or in a New York hotel room: "Sullivan continued to visit him one or two times a week, and often he would spend the evening with the General . . . In the beginning, his bodyguard had thought MacArthur cold and austere, but later he concluded that thus was largely reticence . . . Once Sullivan revealed that he planned to enter a Randall's Island track meet. MacArthur fired him up with a pep talk, ending: 'Don't come back unless you're a winner.' Inspired, the bodyguard broke the track's hammer-throw record and, though he was the oldest man there, he was voted the meet's outstanding athlete. He recalls: 'I think the General could talk *anybody* into *anything.*'"[87]

Also, as does Erickson, Adler and the later Hillman, rhetoric envisions man as essentially, a citizen, a social creature.

Rhetoric viewed man first of all as a social creature. It turned away from the speculative method and ideal of truth in dialectic, seeking rather to find practical, ethical, and political rules for human life and action. But rhetoric could be more than a pragmatic attitude toward man and reality. Its roots have been sought in sophism, which preceded from the idea that reality was eternally changing and that man was the measure of all things. It renounced absolute, objective knowledge of the world, which the philosophers asserted was possible through pure reason and the laws of logic . . . But there was a kind of optimism in the thought that man was a unity of thought, feeling and will . . .

Rhetoric asserted that man was a unity of thought, feeling and will, but it stressed, too, that man acted different roles vis-à-vis his fellow men on the social stage, and, therefore reflected incessantly about his own identity. Finally, it stressed that the personality the listener seemed to find in a speaker often meant more than his argument. This experience inspired both pragmatic and aesthetic speculations about developing an individual style, not only to captivate the public by means of what was idiosyncratic in competition with other artists, but also to express those values and ideals that seemed vital and decisive.[88]

The ideal of rhetoric is to affirm man in his worldliness and to educate him to take his place in the world, to, as Erickson thought, and sounding a lot like Adler, fulfill the basic tasks of life, or with Adler, to develop social interest of which courage is the other side, or with Hillman, to become an eccentric, effective citizen, or with the Thomistic, Dantean approach imagined here, to develop a worldly wisdom that becomes a force for good. And is this so far from Freud's description of the goal of therapy: *"lieben und arbeiten,"* to love and to work?

When inspiration flags, I fall back on Adler and to the encouragement that he made the keystone of his therapy: therapy with responsibility. "Adler never encouraged without laying open the problem for solution of which courage was to be used. Not encouragement in itself but balance of encouragement and responsibility was Adler's formula, if formula there has to be. Therefore he avoided pointing out to the patient tasks which he knew were too difficult for him. His encouragement, furthermore, never meant simply, 'Go ahead you are all right,' but 'Go ahead, if you try very hard you will do it.'"[89] Adlerian encouragement looks back to Nietzsche's recoil from Pearl's like intervention, like confrontation: "Let us stop thinking so much about punishment, reproaching, and improving others! We rarely change an individual, and if we succeed for once, something also may have been accomplished, unnoticed: we may have been changed by him . . . Let us not contend in a direct fight—and that is what all reproaching, punishing and attempts to improve others amount to. Let us raise ourselves that much higher."[90] For me it is always tactful encouragement, that is to say, I tend to pass over lightly fault and flaw to reaffirm virtue, strengths, achievements. Every life brims with them. The human spirit itself, as William Faulkner said so magnificently in his Nobel Prize acceptance speech, will endure and prevail. "By tact," as Gadamer says, "we understand a special sensitivity and sensitiveness to situations and how to behave in them, for which knowledge of general principles does not suffice. Hence an essential part of tact is that it is tacit and unformulable. One can say something tactfully; but that will always mean that one passes over something tactfully and leaves it unsaid, and it is tactless to express what one can only pass over. But to pass over something does not mean to avert one's gaze from it, but to keep an eye on it in such a way that rather than knock into it, one slips by it. Thus tact helps one to preserve distance. It avoids the offensive, the intrusive, the violation of the intimate sphere of the person."[91]

Tact brings feeling into therapy, into this therapeutic approach. Hillman calls tact the crown of feeling: "Tact, or the sense of timing,

is perhaps the crown of appropriate feeling . . . Perhaps feeling is
merely tactfulness, a matter of timing."[92] Tact goes hand in hand with
manners. "The objective patterns of relationship are codified in manners. Learning manners means learning forms of feeling . . . The rediscovery of the archetypal significance of manners as necessary and
viable channels rather than protective moats would re-ritualize them
and give to the careless acts of every day an aspect of ceremony. We
would feel with certainty about the simplest acts of daily life—how to
behave and what is expected. Manners would give us the 'manner' of
dealing . . . manners are archetypally connected with the numinous:
they imply a relation to power. They appear at their most elaborate
where power is concentrated: in the church, the military, the gov-
ernment, or in the contest of powers, e.g., law courts, sports, aboard
ship, in surgery."[93] This is the psychology of Jupiter, of the court, of
the monarch, of Charlemagne: "The Emperor is in a broad orchard,
and with him are Roland and Oliver, the Duke Sansun, and the proud
Anseis, and Gefrey of Anjou, the king's standard bearer. Gerin and
Gerer are with him also, and many others. There are fifteen thousand
from sweet France. The knights are seated on white silk carpets. The
clever and the elderly are amusing themselves at backgammon and
chess; the quick-blooded young men are fencing. Under a pine tree
near an eglantine they have set a throne of gold, and there sits the
King who rules sweet France. His beard is white and his hair is in
full flower. His body is noble and his bearing is princely. If a man
came looking for him, there would be no need to point him out."[94]
This is the psychology of Zeus as Monarch of Olympus, holding court
in Book I of *The Iliad*. It is the psychology of Dante's *Paradisio* and
Castiglione's *The Courtier*, the psychology of Yeats' "A Prayer for My
Daughter": "How but in custom and ceremony / Are innocence and
beauty born? / Ceremony's a name for the rich horn, / And custom

for the spreading laurel tree." It is a psychology and therapy aspiring to be a therapy of encouragement and tact and manners, of great feeling, great sensitivity and refinement, with vision and strategy.

As I aim at reasonableness and chivalry, at a worldly wisdom that is a force for good, so I hope each client will leave armed with a vision and a plan, uplifted and encouraged. This passage from Manes Sperber about counseling with Alfred Adler captures my goal.

> Even after a brief conversation (with Adler) one went away filled with a new faith in oneself, with indistinct but firm hopes for one's own near or distant future—and not because one might thenceforth expect more of others. All of a sudden one realized one had to demand more of oneself, summon up more strength and courage than one had ever thought possible. Many felt that they had become different, better, more intelligent and active members of the human community. And this feeling could last an evening, a day, a week, sometimes longer ... [95]

No therapy is uniformly successful. Nor is any person, which is what brings someone to therapy in the first place. Life disheartens and discourages. What explains this? What cripples a soul, what strips it of its Pauline armor, and robs it of its natural appetites for the gifts and goodness of God's creation? For those luminous moments "when upon the shop and street I gazed / my body of a sudden blazed / For twenty minutes more or less / so great it was my tenderness / that I was blessed and could bless?" What suspends the desire to serve? To belong? To strive? To build one's ship of exploration and of death?

Another way of describing "a worldly wisdom that is a force for good" is *virtu*, as Pound evoked it, or Aristotle, virtue in the Renaissance and Classical sense. The question, then, is what defeats and checkmates virtue? The answer is vice, specifically, vanity—"all neurosis is vanity," said Adler—cowardice, sloth, and ignorance. Clinically, when the clinic is done DSM style, vanity translates into narcissism; cowardice into anxiety; sloth into depression; ignorance into denial. These I reframe as self-consciousness, inexperience, inactivity, and unawareness when it is necessary to address them at all, which is typically only a few times and only in the effort to inspire, encourage, restore morale by learning from mistakes, which I reframe, noble ascription-style, as brave solutions which have outlived their usefulness and like all things that have outlived their usefulness ought to be honorably discharged and retired; and explaining in monologue the reasons for "human unsuccess" (Auden). Why did I fail? Why am I failing? What is happening to me? I'm falling apart. I'm miserable. I don't know what to do. We're all human; all prey to the same mistakes and errors, the same pitfalls. We all have our own private nightmares and demons. We all have feet of clay, backsides and burdens, secrets and blunders. Some few poor souls have real afflictions, illnesses, disease that misshapes their minds and bodies. But these are challenges, not curses, a gauntlet that life has thrown down at your feet. But it is tempting to use them as a crutch. Put down your crutch and walk. And, perhaps . . . perhaps, as corny as it sounds, choose a mission, launch an expedition, set sail, spy your mountain and climb. I don't know whether it's the courage of fools or the courage to be. Don Quixote, Viktor Frankl, the Jesuits in South America, maybe even Richard Burton and Clint Eastwood. *Man of la Mancha*, *Man's Search for Meaning*, *The Mission*, and *Where Eagles Dare*. Sam Houston, while living with the Indians, read *The Iliad*. For Robert Kennedy, after his brother's death, it was Aeschylus. Harold Macmillan, under fire in World War I, read the Stoics, as did William Walker Percy, author of *Lanterns of the Levee*. Me, I'm sort of like that guy in Altman's *Nashville*, I just try to "keep-a-going."

All of this takes place against the background of the fundamentals of therapy. I take it for granted that a therapist is professional and that he understands the basics of his profession, so that the conversation with the patient develops through the establishment of trust and honor that gives a patient sanction to pour out his soul, his miseries and afflictions, but also his shy hungers for transcendence and unbury his dead and buried dreams; to learn the names and promptings of the passions and emotions, his disorders and dysfunctions, his illnesses and trauma, which can be a "seething cauldron," as Freud called the Id, but a crucible—the alchemical vessel as Jung might say—as well; to learn the constructs of his thoughts, his core beliefs, their roots and genesis and sources, their echoes and interdependencies—are we natural Platonists or Aristotelians?—to learn to name the gestalts of his behavior, their repetitive compulsions, of how these patterns sometimes trip us up and throttle our best of intentions; how we desperately repeat them, gradually drawing the noose around our own neck. I take it for granted that conversation generates fresh insight; new ways of being in the world; new candor and strength in speech; that it helps in braving crises; that it yields a richer sense of first and last things.

But the core of what I do, what distinguishes my approach is the trifecta of visioning, strategizing, encouraging. In sessions, even as I practice improvisationally, "guessing" as Adler described it, or, with Haley, encouraging trainees to "go with whatever idea occurs to you," both of which counsels extend the Dantean, Humanistic Renaissance conception of the *ingenium*:

> The special faculty of knowing lies in the *ingenium*, with its help man *collects* the things *which to those who possess no ingenium seem to be without any relationship to one another. Ingenium is* the "grasping," rather than the "deductive" property. The grasp,

however, precedes the deduction because we can draw conclu-
sions only from what we have already grasped. "*Ingenium* is the
faculty to unite what is dispersed and diverse."[96]

This is what I am consciously attempting to do. I throw my heart
over the fence, but I am a mindful rider—*outrider* might be the better word.

How long does therapy last? Sometimes short term—six sessions;
sometimes long term—six months or a year; sometimes, as an exercise in spiritual and psychological growth—many years, to the point,
as Freud anticipated, of being interminable.

I launch it always with a statement written as candidly and comprehensively as I can, detailing operations and logistics, describing
how therapy works and what can be expected.

As to the strictly clinical part of being a counselor, I take it as
a given that the counselor knows the history of his field: classical
psychiatry (the early psychiatrists who often lived on grounds at the
asylum or sanitarium with their patients, saw and described with
great detail the same things that families do today, but hardly ever
any mental health professionals save those at intake in a psychiatric hospital: mental illness, in the raw, over time, unmedicated), the
modern DSM, Freud, Jung and Adler, Hillman and Lacan, Maslow,
Rogers, and May, the great family therapists and systems thinkers;
the cognitive behaviorists, evolutionary biology, neuropsychology,
brain research; but all must be melded, molded by the person that
he is, which means his faith, his losses, his loves, his loyalties, his
attachments and affections, his history, his "sign," his eccentricity.

In addition, it is critical to remember that history does not exist
inside psychology, but psychology exists in history. It is a historical
discipline and hence is best taught and learned as such, including

in its clinical dimension. "What we now know," whatever it is that we think we know, is never more, nor less, than a present knowledge built on a past and shaped by the future that we intend. And as the psyche does not exist in psychology, but psychology exists in the psyche, this historical discipline will always reflect the psyche of the teacher, his "subjective equation."

I once had a physician tell me that he sought out my care instead of seeing a psychiatrist, a fellow M.D., because, he said, "Psychiatrists could not possibly be competent therapists because they don't know the history of psychology and therapy. When would they have time to learn? In medical school they were too busy studying medicine. Not much time left over for the Collected Works of Freud and Jung."

The great literary critic Harold Bloom described romantic poetry as an "internalization of the quest romance." To ask a counselor to assume the role of the *strategos* is to make an unconscious content (the military motifs in analytic and family therapy history) conscious. Therapist as *strategos* represents a psychologizing of Jupiter-Mars constellation. For a Catholic Archetypal Psychology it is vocation and destiny. Most importantly, from my point of view, the image of therapist as *strategos* fulfills a Thomistic-Dantean psychological project and answers Reinhold Schneider's call, the answering of which he believed to be the West's last hope, for what he called a "spiritualization of chivalry."

HOUSEHOLD GODS

> Early in 1934, he and Chesterton were appointed by the Pope
> Knights of the Order of St. Gregory the Great. "Aren't you go-
> ing to answer your letter from the Pope, Mr. Belloc?" . . . "Why
> should I accept an honor from some greasy Monsignore?" . . . the
> rebuff reveals a deeper and harder cynicism in Belloc's nature
> . . . With a part of himself, he was perhaps a pagan, a noble old
> Roman pre-Christian . . . These sides of his mind and imagina-
> tion were held in check by a strong habit of piety. They were
> subsumed and christened.
>
> —A. N. Wilson, *Hilaire Belloc*

In addition to visioning, strategizing, and encouraging, a therapist
models. From the books on the shelves, the pictures on the wall and
desk, the choice of furniture, the manner of decor, the sparkle or dull-
ness of the imagination, every practice expresses the person of the
therapist, his loves and loyalties, his affections and affiliations.

This, too, is the way of the *strategos*. General Mathew Taylor
("Kennedy's General") writes: "Professional competence is more
than a display of book knowledge or of the results of daily schooling.
It requires the display of qualities of character which reflect inner
strength and justify confidence in one's self. To give an impression
of strength an officer must consider his personal appearance, his
physical condition, his tone of voice, his style of life—all of which
give an impression of his character."[97] "For all the insouciance of his
demeanor, MacArthur remained as attentive to his image as ever.
Like his hero, Napoleon, once he had established a totemic picture
of himself as the most resplendent figure in uniform, he suddenly

enfolded himself in a simplicity equally extreme, equally noticeable . . . MacArthur chose to have legend ornament his chest."[98]

If you ask me who I am—What do I model? What is my "nature"?

First, what the Jungians might call my shadow. My sins are scarlet. My faults are many. My clinical judgment is sometimes simply wrong. I have an outsized ego that often remains invisible to me. I sometimes talk down to people. I can be overbearing, overly optimistic, excessively didactic, impatient to get to the point. I'm over-defended and intellectualize. I've been called "critical, arrogant, aloof, and distant" (the acronym is caad) which in my over-defended way I defend as merely being shy and introverted. I'm embarrassingly narcissistic at times, of which this entire exercise might be an example. On the other hand someone once said that the real title of every book ought to be "Title: Or How To Be More Like Me." My writings, which have often explored loss, my own and others, have too often softened loss with poetry—"emotion recollected in tranquility," as Wordsworth said. Loss is never poetic. It is ineffably ugly, cold, blunt, savage. I do say truly with the Roman centurion, "Lord I am not worthy to receive you, but only say the word and I shall be healed."

My shadow leaked into my training. As Adler said, "No one suffers subordination willingly." In a temperamental way, this is undeniably true in my case. I have been a case. I underwent a brief training analysis—nine months as I remember—with James Hall, an accomplished Jungian analyst and a tragic figure whose individuation journey brought him to the Catholic Church. At his invitation I participated as a guest in his training group. From an analytic point of view I broke off the analysis prematurely. From my point of view it had run its course. The vigor of the intellect and teaching of the phenomenologist Robert Romanyshyn first attracted me to psychology. Classes and conversations with the spiritual psychologist, Robert

Sardello, were a critical part of my formation. Sardello is the only true genius I have ever met. I recall him being urgently asked "what to do?" about a particularly trying psychiatric inpatient case. In response he said: "The first thing to do is think about it." Genuinely sage advice. For a half dozen years I was an assistant to James Hillman (see Coda of the present volume). Whatever training I received from him was limited to his example. In conversations and a written exchange or two, Patricia Berry by her example and words challenged me to a clarity that would not forsake depth. Berry's "when-then" construct for dream interpretation may be said to be a systemic approach to the dream. The "when-then" construct was easily adaptable to the family—"when Dad does this, Mom does this and the identified patient, the child, does this." It certainly smoothed my transition into the family therapy world. At this stage of my career, it seems more accurate to describe the "when-then" idea as the foundation for an archetypal psychology approach to working with families. Dr. Heinz Ansbacher, Adler's chief interpreter, encouraged my Adlerian work and "mentored" me though a year's worth of correspondence. Ansbacher's most sobering comment was that he "could not do what I could do" as a therapist and therein lay the weakness, the Achilles heel, of my approach. It could not be taught nor replicated. I did a year-long live supervision externship in structural-strategic therapy at the Salesmanship Club which at the time was (still is) a cutting-edge training center which now often operates conjointly with the Houston-Galveston Family Therapy Center, where constructivist post modern therapy was born, as the Reunion Institute.

As far as my shadow affecting the direction I'm taking? My father saw combat in two wars; retired as a lieutenant Colonel in the Marine Corp. Freud said happiness is fulfilling a childhood wish; one of my fondest childhood memories is playing Stratego, a sort of poor man's chess. I grew up preparing to apply to the Air Force Academy; played football until injured, excelled academically, made Student Council and Vice President of the National Honor Society. My father knew the local Congressman and talked to him about an appointment. 1967—the Summer of Love—swept all that away, along with my relationship to my Dad, not mended fully until the last years of his life. Father wound; childhood wish, unfulfilled ambition; craving combat to test my insecure masculinity? Perhaps. Perhaps I just want to be Emperor.

If I were to teach a course attempting to combine clinical training with personal growth—with the insight into one's own soul that Freud insisted is the primary analytic qualification—I would use George Patton's two-volume *The Patton Papers 1885-1940*, a collection of letters, diary excerpts, reflections, as an example of the unflinching self-appraisal of which these last three paragraphs are a poor imitation. These two books would furnish the primary texts together with Robert H. Patton's (Patton's grandson) very sensitive and sharply critical story of the Patton family, *The Pattons*.

By grace and conversion, I'm Roman Catholic. I'm Roman in sympathies—Roman in contrast to Greek; Norse and Norman by blood, with a touch of the Celt and Saxon. The only ancestor whom I can directly trace was a 16th century Frenchman. I was born in Dallas, Texas part of whose history begins, wondrously enough, in France, with French utopians. Texas is South by Southwest, but my family roots are in East Texas where I spent a lot of time growing up. East Texas is as Southern as Mississippi.

I've dug deep into the American Old South, to end with, as did Allen Tate, one of our most brilliant exegetes and exponents, an uneasy feeling that the Old Jeffersonian, Aristocratic, Agrarian South, though it did maintain much of the High Tradition, was nonetheless weakened by a false mythology and riddled not only with the abomination of slavery but a greedy acquisitive energy, as all-consuming as that which existed in the Hamiltonian, Industrial, Capitalist North.

To be sure, however, though supremely conscious of all our sins, I am proud to be a Southerner. As Bernard-Henry Levy writes in his *American Vertigo*: "All right, I've changed my mind. If I had to take up residence in one city in this country—if I had to choose one town and only one to live in—it might not be Seattle after all, but Savannah. Savannah's allure. Its striking, Old South beauty . . . this refined Savannah, infused with aristocratic value, where, I am convinced, this very aristocracy, this art of living and this taste for art in life, more so than slavery itself, inspired Northern resentment."[99]

As a Southerner I dream, of course. We're all in our souls front porch dreamers at dusk, with moon glow and magnolia, fireflies flitting on the lawn, of a South that rises again, rises not in battle but in cultural renaissance, as it already has, of course, in the Southern Literary Renaissance—what is indeed the glamour of New York without Southern writers, without Wolfe, Williams and Capote?—but not as Faulkner's every Southern 14 year-old boy would have it, of a Southern victory at Gettysburg, nor as it rose up gigantic in the anguished eyes of W. J. Cash who saw in Atlanta's soaring, rising skyline the thundering ghosts of Stuart's Cavalry. My dream is born in the humbling, penitent realization that "The South's religious mind was inarticulate, dissenting, and schismatical. She had a non-agrarian and trading religion that had been invented in the sixteenth century by a young finance-capitalist economy: hardly a religion at all but rather a disguised secular ambition."[100] As Nietzsche dreamt of a re-Latinized North, I dream of a Latinized Catholic South, of French and Spanish ghosts and flags that still haunt our sacred ground and history; of New Orleans, our archetypal city— " . . . that city foreign and para-

doxical, with its atmosphere at once fatal and languorous, at once
feminine and steel hard . . . a place whose denizens had created their
All-Powerful and His supporting hierarchy-chorus of beautiful saints
and handsome angels in the image of their houses and personal ornaments and voluptuous lives."[101] A tortured city that must be reborn if
it is to survive. My dream is born in the stubborn story of Washington, like James II, converting to Catholicism on his deathbed; in Mr.
Jefferson who often said he preferred France to all other countries. It
is fed from the sentiments of Southern Cavaliers like James Johnston
Pettigru, known in his time as "the most promising young man in the
South" and who, as a South Carolinian General was at the head of
his troops in Pickett's Charge, only to die, gut shot, during the army's
retreat back across the Potomac. Prior to the war, Pettigru travelled
Southern Europe, where the journals that he kept evolved into an
extraordinary, privately printed book. As he entered Italy Pettigru
wrote: " . . . my feeling of satisfaction arose; I felt as I used to do leaving the Yankee land on the way to the South. At almost every railway
station, one could perceive an increase in the beauty of the women,
in the sociability of the men, and in the smiling genial aspect of the
country."[102] Of Spain: "For my own part I confess to a decided par-
tiality for many things in it. I like the flowery vales of Andalusia and
the tawny mountains of Aragon. I like to kneel in its Cathedrals and
to promenade by moonlight upon its Paseos. I like to ride in its dili-
gences when I have a place in the berlina. I like its prancing horses
and pawing bulls. I like its fandangos and its *olés*, its guitars and its
wild, plaintive melodies. I like its oranges and pomegranates. I like its
marble courts and sparkling fountains. I like its dry, invigorating cli-
mate. I like its language. I like its punctilious, brave and elegant men.
But far above all these do I adore its women—the immortal, the ever-
beautiful!"[103] In Italy and Spain Pettigru discovered the older Roman

civilization with which his own world had so achingly much in common, and by whose consonance with which so dramatically differed
from the North. "Was it imagination? . . . Was it reality? Elsewhere in
Europe there was little to compensate for the moss-draped oaks, the
sweet-smelling magnolias, the flowering vines of my own home: for
the sensitive honor running at times into extremes, which is yet the
main-spring to the character of a gentleman: for the enthusiasm, sin-
cerity and gentle nature of our beautiful women. All these had a place
in my recollection of Spain . . . "[104] As Pettigru remembered Spain, so
my dream imagines Norman Sicily as flower and type of such a civilization. Sicily, perhaps, on the day of Roger II's, the first King—and
a Norman King at that—of Sicily, crowning: " . . . henceforth Sicily
seems to radiate a new confidence, a new awareness of her place in
Europe and of the mission she has to fulfil. The chronicles became
fuller and more informative; the characters recover their flesh and
blood; and the cultural genius that was Norman Sicily's chief legacy
to the world bursts at last into the fullness of its flower."[105] Roger II,
as Robert D. Kaplan notes, "was a strategic genius."[106]

Before East Texas was Southern, it was French. LaSalle, St. Denis,
Lafitte. I would recommend a biography of St. Denis, *Cavalier in the
Wilderness*, by Ross Phares, to give a flavor of this. Of the six flags
that have flown over Texas, the French may have been the best. The
French came not to settle or conquer, even for Christ; they came to
trade and blend in and later to pirate.

At the source, whether French or Southern, East Texas was always
Cavalier, not much Cowboy.

If there is an unacknowledged shade standing behind my work
it is Robert Desoille, French psychologist and educator, whose as-
pirational, ascensional, image-rich directive psychology I've studied,
taught, been influenced by, and revere. In the technique of the Direct-

ed Daydream, Desoille projected generous visions, full of clouds and mountains, brightness and light, in which he invited his patients to imaginatively participate. As already suggested with hypnosis and all activist or strategic therapeutic techniques, the Directed Daydream is the translation into a clinical technique of rhetoric. In this case it is the old rhetorical, Classical and Renaissance Idea of Grandeur, the lofty literary style of splendor and magnificence. It is a technique and a style whose purpose is to foster the sublime. Desoille's idea that the goal of psychotherapy is to engender magnanimity accords with my own. Further, the passage to magnanimity occurs through a gracious guidance—"tactful encouragement"—on the part of the therapist that glides past the painful and embarrassing, whatever burns with conflict and contradiction, so that the patient may attain a new perspective, one befitting his greater magnanimity.

Whether done with greater or lesser degree of collaboration, whether called interpretation, reframing or re-narration, all therapy involves the re-telling of a patient's story into a more satisfying form. From a Desoillean point of view, the best interpretation would be the one that elevates, something that family therapy discovered early on, so that structural strategic therapists began to speak of "noble ascriptions." The best interpretation is the one that in Yeatsian fashion ennobles "looking for the Face you had / Before the world was made." The best interpretation is the one that most augments truth (meaning), goodness (value), beauty (appeal). So, too, the best philosophy and psychology.

I cannot say that I built on Desoille. My study was not that intensive, though I did employ the Directed Daydream for many years in therapy. But exposure to Desoille did set me on the road of thinking of an archetypal psychology that could be *sui generis* shorn away from its Jungian baggage. This would be an archetypal psychology that could be a genuine craft, an art, an activist, interventionist form of life, letters, and therapy. The Jungian mystique of the analyst as priest, shaman, witness, observer, confessor, midwife, etc. never temperamentally suited me and seemed an exercise in Sartrean bad faith. The same goes for all the non-directive, collaborative, therapist as witness, facilitator views that appeal to the Socratic mid-wife ideal. If you have ever seen a Socratic Dialogue performed, you quickly realize that Socrates is the only one who talks. Everyone else is reduced to playing Ed McMahon-like straight man to Johnny Carson on the old Tonight show: "Yes, Socrates." "No, Socrates." "You're absolutely right, Socrates." A gifted psychotherapist once described to me her analysis with the famous Jungian analyst, Marie Louise von Franz. "I would go and tell her a dream, and then she would talk for an hour." My analyst certainly talked a good deal, gave me advice and directed me to do things which I assume he believed to be strategic, although he would never have used the word—strategic in being economical, efficient, maybe elegant or at least something other than a royal waste of time. I would argue that the image of therapist as *strategos* allows a productive re-thinking of Jungian analysis as a strategic attempt to foster the symbolic life and soul making. Understood in this way, and at this level of conceptualization, perhaps I am a Catholic Jungian psychologist—the symbolic life and soul-making, like the Mass, the Rosary and Confession good strategies for serving God. (A very Bellocian and Norman way of looking at things, incidentally.) As his biographer notes, responding to Malcolm Muggeridge's description of Belloc as "there being very little religion in him": "This would certainly be true if by 'religion' is meant pious conversation, or an overt discussion of spirituality. It was contrary to Belloc's nature to be slushily pious; still less could he have boasted about the extent of his own spiritual enlightenment."[107] Analyst as

Pontifex Maximus, a title the Popes took from the Roman Emperors—Julius II again.

Desoille ended his career as a Communist. I approach the end of mine as a traditionalist conservative Catholic. There's analogy here, not irony. Jay Haley once mused that the reason family therapy was originally most successful in Italy, rather than the States, is because in Italy all the clients were either Communists or Catholics—both groups accepted authority.

What these identities and origins mean, is that to tell you who I am is to tell you what I do rather than what I think or believe. Catholics, Romans, Normans tend to be practical, pragmatic people. It is, therefore, to tell you what Rule I live by. I do live by a certain Rule, or try to, at the heart of which is Mass, the Rosary, and Confession. What I eat mostly are soups and stews and salads, bread, coffee and wine—being, at times, "one of those Catholic men," whom Belloc preferred, "who live upon wine." I try to stay fit. I've always liked long slow jogs in the early morning, when the air is fresh and the stars just fading or along back country roads, sweet with pine scent, honeysuckle and magnolia, hazy with the Texas summer and waves of heat. I dabble at the edge of the Martial Arts as an episodic practitioner, not a spectator. I started when I was sixteen. I studied in the old Jefferson Street dojo, where Skipper Mullens, one of karate's all time greats, was my instructor. The first time I ever sparred it was with Demetrius Havanas, the "Golden Greek," who quickly taught me what a champion was and that I wasn't going to be one. At the time he was only a Blue Belt. The Martial Art that most interests me is Savate. I make a fair amount of money, but never charging more than a patient can fairly bear. My economics are Distributist, but, like Belloc, I covet cash.

The writers I read mostly now are Hilaire Belloc and Frederick D. Wilhelmsen, into whose work I regularly dip for inspiration and strength. I relish Histories, especially military, manuals of strategy, and anything about the Normans. Belloc commemorates them,

> . . . those bullet-headed men, vivacious, and splendidly brave, we know that they awoke all Europe, that the first provided settled financial systems and settled governments of land, and that everywhere, from the Grampians to Mesopotamia, they were like steel when all other Christians were like wood or like lead.
>
> We know that they were a flash. They were not formed or definable at all before the year 1000; by the year 1200 they were gone. Some odd transitory phenomenon of cross breeding, a very lucky freak in the history of the European family, produced the only body of men who were all lords and who in their collective action showed continually nothing but genius.[108]

The Norman myth sustained the Cavalier South.

> Much of the enthusiasm for a rapid Southern victory was rooted in several vague but broadly held nineteenth-century perceptions. Of particular importance was the "Virginia mystique" which seemed to be a means to intimidate the South's opponents. This psyche arose from the popular belief that the Virginian was bred of a superior "cavalier" heritage. In many Old South novels Virginians had long been stereotyped as planter descendants of the Norman aristocrats who ruled Europe for centuries. Such breeding, it was alleged, "perpetuated manly virtues: refined manners, aristocratic behavior, and a strong sense of honor. Above all else, Virginia cavaliers were characterized by gentlemanly martial skills . . . "[109]

Also Churchill, or the Southern Generals Lee, MacArthur ("I am of Virginia" MacArthur wrote to Douglas Southall Freeman), and

Patton. The recent (November 2009) Apostolic Constitution in which the Pope acknowledges the validity of the Anglican Rite and the treasure of Anglican spirituality consoles me because it makes possible to embrace the heroes of blood, sweat, and tears of Britain and of the High Anglican South as brothers in arms with the ancient Catholic chivalry. With Alfred, Charlemagne and Roland, Baldwin, IV, the Leper-King, the Cid, the Bonnie Prince, Count von Stauffenberg. "And there was death on the Emperor / And night upon the Pope / And Alfred, hiding in deep grass / Hardened himself with hope" (Chesterton). I anachronistically enjoy the newspapers the *New York Times*, the *Financial Times*, the *Wall Street Journal*, the *Dallas Morning News*. Van Morrison, Chet Baker, Sinatra and Bennett, also Mozart, Bach, Puccini: this is the music I listen to, listening to Mozart's *Requiem* almost daily.

A word about Belloc and Wilhelmsen: The best summation of Hilaire Belloc, historian, essayist, economist, political theorist, author of 153 books, comes from Wilhelmsen:

> Belloc was not built to fit any cloth fashioned by mortal man . . .
> Belloc was a paradox: a lyrical poet who never read any contemporary poetry, a rhymester whose hijinks still charm children; an artilleryman on bivouac at Toul who smelled the Revolution as "France went by"; an aging monarchist who savored the last charge of Charles I at Naseby; the most versatile and certainly the finest English prose stylist in this and possibly any century . . . the enemy of the rich and capitalist greed who once asked for a bucket of money as a birthday gift; the passionate advocate of Truth who once groused "the truth always limps . . . "[110]

The best appraisal of Wilhelmsen, metaphysician, epistemologist, essayist, cultural historian, co-editor of *Triumph*, and founding board member of *Modern Age*, comes from Patrick Allitt's fine book *Catholic Intellectuals and Conservative Politics in America, 1950-1985*:

> Wilhelmsen believed that the Middle Ages had been an era of luminous clarity and intellectual brilliance . . . but (he) appears to have had relatively little influence among Catholic philosophers or conservative authors early in the 1950s or subsequently . . . Despite his brilliantly acute intellect and internally consistent vision, there was not much support for a man such as Wilhelmsen in contemporary America.[111]

Sadly, then, as now. But for those of us who took his classes—Metaphysics, Medieval Philosophy, Aesthetics—or heard his lectures (dazzling dramas that made philosophy live as if we were in Paris at the great debates between Sigar de Brabant and St. Thomas) and read his essays hot off the press in *Triumph*, when he was Catholic America's most eloquent, inspired interpreter, it was a once-in-a-lifetime experience.

In films I prefer the epics: great heroes and love stories: Charleton Heston in *Ben Hur*; *The Warlord*; *El Cid*, especially; *Out of Africa*; *Robin and Marion*. Today Russell Crowe is my favorite actor. I like *Gladiator, Cinderella Man, Master and Commander* with its beautiful score. *Patton* is my favorite movie, especially the Director's cut, with Francis Ford Coppola providing commentary about understanding that the soul of Patton resided in his sense of himself as a Southern Gentleman, steeped in history and culture and practicing the chivalric art of war. My guilty pleasure is the *Godfather* trilogy. (But it is not really guilty. The *Godfather* films are supremely Catholic, the great twentieth-century epic of the Italian Catholic immigration. It is the story of two terribly flawed men, Vito and Michael, trying to keep honor and family intact in an infernal and purgatorial America. The trilogy ends, as did Dante's *Divine Comedy,* with a Beatrician vision of redemption through love).

My favorite poet is David Jones; my favorite poem, "The Wind-hover" by Gerard Manley Hopkins: "Brute beauty, valor, act, oh air, pride, plume here / Buckle! AND the fire that breaks from Thee then, a billion / Times more lovelier, more, dangerous, Oh my Chevalier!"

My politics are vaguely and uncomfortably Democratic but I have a weakness for Republican populists. My politics are based on the Catholic teaching that the family rather than the individual is the basic unit of society. I look at politics from the perspective of what is best for the family and what is always best for the family is economic fairness, ideally independence. The Democrats do a better job at that. I suppose I would say that I'm a Kennedy Democrat.

For some conservative Catholics, sympathy for the Democrats equates with sympathy for the Devil. Like many others, they deplore the growing power of the Presidency. But as Belloc saw, and endorsed, the American system is more monarchical than the British. America is Rome, as both Belloc and Charles Olson realized. "For the American has the Roman feeling about the world."[112] And what made Rome is the genius of unity of command, centralized authority, the growing power of the executive branch. The difference between Democrat and Federalists-Whigs-Republican is ultimately the difference between two kinds of sovereigns. Democrats are not Jacobins; we're Jacobites, loyalists to a Popular Monarchy, a Patriot King, who with subtlety (Jefferson), ferocity (Jackson), suavity (Roosevelt) or glamour (John F. Kennedy) stands, now firm, now flexible, against the Hamiltonian System, Wall Street and the oligarchy, the banks and "the business interest," corporations and monopolies, against the "Money Power" as the Tory Bolingbroke first described it, the Bolingbroke who was with Swift, Jefferson's favorite author. "Only monarchy can stand

8rt8d8

against Money," said Napoleon. Melville thought Andrew Jackson "had been hurled higher than a throne." And the canard that Democrats are somehow "soft on defense": who overcame the Barbary Pirates, the British in New Orleans, Hitler in World War II, who stood down the Russians in Cuba?

As the family is the basic unit of society for Catholics, so for a Catholic man marriage and family must be the cornerstone of his life: to be partner, protector, provider, and a kind of priest. This is the Old Roman idea of father as military, economic, and spiritual head of the family. It is what I aim at. It's what I aspire to, but fail. After all, we are all shipwrecked men, none of us get out alive, except, as Wilhelmsen says, graves don't exist for Catholics, or better said, they exist only so we can crawl out of them.

The best source, or at least, the best source that I have found, for understanding not what it means to be a Catholic Husband and Father, but what it means, to passionately and vulnerably, try, is Sigrid Undset's great trilogy, *Sigrid Lavransdatter*, in her depiction of Erlend.

Of Erlend, Andrew Lytle says:

> Erlend's love of the world is not unlike Brother Edvin's. The priest's love is the worship of God through God's artifacts, as he said, the ways themselves. With Erlend the ways sank into the marrow of his bones, into all the passages of nerves and flesh which only nature's instinctive, untranslatable language understands. He is at ease everywhere, under all circumstances, for he always knows where he is, at sea, upon the icy wastes, in the mountains, at court, among men. Events do not mar or interrupt his habits formed out of this mysterious inner vision.[113]

Erlend is the father, the feudal lord, the seigneur, the Don, the *pater familias*, who brought low by circumstance, never fulfils his destiny, attains his state, his rightful place. As father, he shows his mettle in innumerable ways. He is firm and gentle, a natural leader; men take to him at once and follow. No one can keep up with him on skis, so he imperceptibly slows his pace that an older man is not left behind. The strength and endurance he shows on skis, he displays during his imprisonment for attempting a plot to restore the Kingdom to its rightful independence. Not thought to be a serious man, he surprises others with his deep knowledge of the law and precedent. All but forgotten by all who know him, is the fact that he served as the King's Warden, a task he did well. After sudden swordplay, he distinguishes himself from his wife's jilted suitor by carefully cleaning the sword before replacing it in its scabbard. Erlend embodies graciousness and gentleness, strength and endurance, wisdom and knowledge, but all but his father-in-law fail to see that his failure to mature lies not with him but with the men who should have been his fathers. They lack the necessary stature:

> Lavrans is judging, as they talk to the High Steward, the chieftain who should have taken over Erlend. Lavrans thought the steward was not big enough even in size to be the chieftain all would follow. He seemed not to fill his seat fully. Upright, prudent, knightly, willing to serve faithfully, he was somewhat too small to be the first man in the realm. The first man must be one to absorb all who can be made to serve the welfare of the land.[114]

The challenges bulk large. As Charles Peguy, the great Catholic poet and social activist, wrote:

> There is only one adventurer in the world, as can be seen very clearly in the modern world, the father of a family. Even the most desperate adventurers are nothing compared with him

. . . Everything is against him. Savagely organized against him. Everything turns and combines against him. Men, events, the events of society, the automatic play of economic laws. And, in short, everything else. Everything is against the father of a family, the *pater familias*; and consequently against the family. He alone is literally "engaged" in the world, in the age. He alone is the adventurer.[115]

I once heard Louise Cowan, one of the great teachers and "new criticism" literary critics of the last century, ask "Are we really, as women, better off now that Marlena Dietrich has been replaced by Cher who has been replaced by Madonna?" Today she might add Lady Gaga.

Adler said that the therapist assumes the maternal function. Nathaniel Ackerman embraced the idea of family therapist as parent. Carl Whitaker called therapists foster parents. Minuchin liked to think of himself joining with the family as if he were a distant uncle visiting for a time. A General cares for and about his troops: "If you read the pages of history with reflection, you find that no man ever rose to military greatness who did not succeed in convincing his troops that he put them first, above all else . . . The successful commander claims no infallibility, and is not afraid to expose himself to close view. Instead he is often seen among his men; he learns their surnames and calls them by name at every opportunity. It is said of Caesar that he never lacked a pleasant word for his soldiers. He remembered the face of anyone who had done a gallant deed, and when not in the presence of the enemy encouraged amusements in which he frequently joined. Such little human acts as these inspired his legionaries with a devotion which went far to account for his success."[116] This sympathetic understanding is definitive for the giving of advice that, notwithstanding all the casuistries that contest this, counseling amounts to. As Gadamer shows, such understanding depends on a shared vision of what is right and a shared feeling too, a shared vulnerability. "The man of the world, the man who knows all the tricks and dodges and is experienced in everything there is, does not really have sympathetic understanding . . . he has it only if he satisfies one requirement, namely that he too is seeking what is right . . . Both the person asking for advice and the person giving it are bound together in friendship . . . Once again we discover that the person who is understanding does not know and judge as one who stands apart and unaffected but rather he thinks along with the other from the perspective of a specific bond of belonging, as if he too were affected."[117] This is Jupiterian. *The Odyssey* begins with Zeus proclaiming the difference between right and wrong and *The Iliad* with Thetis beseeching Zeus who is moved and nods his assent to her plea. Such vision and emotion characterizes men under this archetypal sign. Churchill: "Hitler was much less emotional than Churchill. His personality was cold . . . Churchill's was warm. No one had ever seen a tear in Hitler's eyes, whereas tears would often gather in Churchill's, which seemed not to have bothered or shamed him at all."[118] So, too, MacArthur: "For MacArthur, anything worth feeling was worth feeling deeply, and it was honest emotion, freely expressed, that was the cement of real life, the stuff that held the bric-a-brac of daily existence together and gave it shape and meaning. His temperament was that of the poet, the artist, the thinker, as well as the man of action."[119]

For a Roman Catholic counselor practicing under the Dantean archetypal sign of Jupiter, for a *strategos* whose primary responsibility is to care for and care about his troops, this would be the father's role, the *pater familias*, the father whose role it is to be the military, economic, and spiritual head of the family, the father whose comfort is evoked by the stunningly beautiful dream that concludes Cormac McCarthy's *No Country for Old Men*, where the hardscrabble sheriff dreams of his father riding past him, with fire in the horn, to go ahead to make camp. It is an old image, familiar to hunters, with powerful Biblical resonance. In *Out of Africa*, Isak Dinesen explains her leaving Africa for Denmark in similar fashion: she will go ahead, as is done in the bush when hunting, to make camp, and light a fire so that others may find her. As Our Lord said, "I go to prepare a place for you."

So as a Roman Catholic counselor, a strategic family therapist and archetypal psychologist, I vision, strategize, encourage, model, and try to give comfort too, listening, empathizing, consoling, comforting, caring. Cormac McCarthy furnishes a beautiful image for this part of therapy.

THE KING'S GREAT HORN

Fealty, piety, loyalty, the swearing of allegiance, the pledging of swords, and the bending of the knee—these are the realities that are always playing out their chivalric drama in the back of my consciousness, and neither doctrine nor polity that fails to place them to the forefront can ever receive from me more than a passing curiosity, or half-hearted attention.
—Frederick D. Wilhelmsen, "Why I am a Catholic"

My medieval knees lack health until they bend.
—W. B. Yeats

Here as elsewhere, now as in the past, writing for me, as therapy is, has always been excursional. I've always written for an audience, not for the ages. I'm a rhetor, not a scholar. As a rhetor, you always tune to someone else's key, which is, of course, the daily task of a therapist, a practical reason for exploring rhetoric.

I've spoken of rhetoric. Let me add to that here. The traditional definition of rhetoric is eloquent language that seeks to "teach, move, please." Another, slightly more contemporary way to put this might be that a rhetorical approach is one that attempts to educate, inspire, and delight, which it does through strong, bold statements and quotations, firm and soaring rhythms—as Yeats said, "the rhythm of a man on horseback"—and sensuous, dramatic, memorable imagery. At its peak this is what was once called "Ciceronian rhetoric." From Classical Rome to Renaissance Court, learned Humanists aspired to such eloquence. It flowed naturally from the pen of Andrew Jackson:

Jackson wrote with a vigorous scrawl that reflected the strength of his character. Admittedly, his sentences collide with each other, running on line after line in a wild "Ciceronian" style; ideas crowd against each other in a rapid, free flow of thought; commas, dashes, or pauses replace periods; and all manner of grammatical mayhem savage the English language. Nonetheless, despite the lapses, he commanded a powerful style of writing. His prose sometimes vibrated with all the energy and aggressiveness of his forceful and explosive personality. He wrote as he talked: strong, assertive, self-confident. His imagery, especially when he got himself worked up, conveyed enough raw power to jolt readers even a hundred and fifty years after it was written. When he communicated with Spanish governors or Indian chieftains, for example, he frequently summoned an eloquence of unparalleled thrust and drive.[120]

It is Southern style of speech. As Tate said, "The traditional Southern mode of discourse presupposes somebody at the other end silently listening: it is the rhetorical mode."[121] Jefferson, too, promoted the music of language over the pedantry of grammar. "It may be noted by way of analogy that if he was a strict constructionist with respect to the American Constitution he was certainly not one with regard to English grammar. When President, he asked Madison to read and revise his first annual message to Congress, saying: 'Where strictness of grammar does not weaken expression, it should be attended to in complaisance to the purists of New England. But where by small grammatical negligences, the energy of an idea is condensed, or a word stands for a sentence, I hold grammatical rigor in contempt.' More than a score of years later . . . he told this learned young New Englander that he was not 'an adept in the metaphysical speculations of Grammar,' nor 'a friend to a scrupulous purism of style.' Instead he readily sacrificed 'the niceties of syntax to euphony and strength.'"[122] I would call it Southern, yes, and Yeatsian, Faulknerian, Wilhelmsenian and Hillmanian—James Hillman being surely the finest prose stylist psychology has produced. At its pits it is purple prose. Whether I learned this style by emulating styles I loved, or, whether, it comes naturally; whether it is "constructivist" or "expressionistic"; it is the style in which my thought develops, my imagination takes shape, in which my sentences go forward.

Although addressed to audiences, it seems to me now that my writing has always harkened back towards the High Middle Ages. The path has not been straight, but it has been onward. During the twentieth-century Catholic Literary Renaissance in the English speaking world (Belloc, Chesterton, the historian Christopher Dawson, the poet David Jones, the sculptor Eric Gill; Gilson and Maritain, once they were in the States; the poets Allen Tate, Kenneth Rexroth, William Everson; Dorothy Day and Peter Maurin and the Catholic Worker movement; Marshall McLuhan and Wilhelmsen) it was often asserted that the High Middle Ages were a time of "reasonableness and chivalry" far surpassing our own. "Medieval man sacramentalized the whole of being," declares Wilhelmsen. If I may be forgiven for quoting myself:

> The Medieval Church was a Church of miracles, mystery plays and Marian devotion and a sense of a world steeped in Mary's presence. It was a Church of prayer and pilgrimage, of relics and rituals, of county fairs and sacred processions, a Church with a frank sensuality and bawdy sexuality, a Church of Saints and feast days, of Christmas and May Day . . .
>
> It was a Church whose spires stormed heaven, whose philosophy was brilliant, whose theology shone glory and whose ratio-

nal defense of a universal and intelligible nature prepared the
way for modern science, as even Whitehead acknowledges . . .

And finally through its sacramentalization of the order of
chivalry, the Medieval Church restrained and chastened the vio-
lence of human nature, while converting its strength, not only
into a force for good, but also a shield for the weak . . . [123]

I suggested earlier that most of us are either Greek or Roman. A
better classification might be Classical or Middle Ages, Renaissance
or Enlightenment, Modern or Post-Modern. The journals abound
now with articles about post-modernism. I'm not only not post-modern; I'm positively medieval.

Published in Jungian journals, and written under the influence of
James Hillman, my early essays on alchemy reflect this. I sensed, early on, taking classes from Wilhelmsen, the need for a medieval psychology that was a lyrical, chivalric, sacramental view of the world
that was nonetheless rigorously intellectual. In Jungian psychology,
especially as represented in the work of James Hillman and his early
colleague Evangelos Christou, I initially seemed to find it. My dis-
sertation and essays on Adler intuited and tried to work out, with
the tools I then had available, the idea that both Adler and Nietzsche
were counter-revolutionary, even counter-Reformation thinkers.
Through Adler's work reverberates Civitas, even Romanitas; through
Nietzsche's work, it is chivalry. Nietzsche's first memory, upon which
an Adlerian would put great stock diagnostically, reprises the myth of
Percival. My essay on Courage, which wore the garb of an Adlerian
approach addressed to the Men's Movement, was in truth the evo-
cation of a Catholic courage, "the courage of fools." As Chesterton
wrote: "But you and all the kind of Christ / Are ignorant and brave,
/ And you have wars you hardly win / And souls you hardly save."
Another book, *Charms and Rituals*, reaches to a medieval psychol-

ogy, written to my great joy and freedom, as an almost medieval book, a garden of stories, parables, poetry, insights, images, history etc. It was half jongleur, half Anton Mesmer. I then wrote dozens of essays, some of which are collected in my *Adoption: Philosophy and Experience*, and little books—*Can't You Sit Still?*; *A Mighty Time*; *Family Preservation; Love and Discipline*, whose intention was to both exemplify and encourage "reasonableness and chivalry" that is a worldly wisdom that is a force for good. Next, *Spiritual Existential Counseling*, a Chestertonian book, inspired by the radiance and fire of the "Glorious Doctor," the greatest theologian of the twentieth century, Cardinal Hans Urs von Balthasar, that most clearly represents my approach. Then, an unpublished book, *A Southern Gentleman's Psychology* that grappled with the Norman-Cavalier-Virginian mystique that infused my upbringing and formal education. Marshall McLuhan called it "That Southern Quality." As he attests in the brilliant essay of the same title, "It was no mere archeological revival. It has the full vitality of medieval chivalry and courtly love in every part of it." Most recently, though even that some years ago, "A Catholic Therapy: Description and Epistemology" delivered at the annual meeting of The Society for Catholic Social Science.

Finally, it is against the background of the medieval world that even this writing—I always liked the poet David Jones' refusal to distinguish between genres, insisting that even *The Anathemata*, called by Auden "the greatest long poem of the century" be called a "writing"—makes sense and comes to close a kind of circle with all that I've written in years past, which, as I've said, often explore loss; and with a personal life that, for all its joys, has partaken of at least its fair share of tragedy. As Wilhelmsen writes:

The life of men in those centuries was the life of the soldier . . . In those days the *Te Deum* was the hymn of marching soldiers and the hair shirt was often worn under chain mail. Knights Templars, before their decline and suppression, slept in open graves the better to prepare themselves for the nervous scimitars and delicate mounts of Islam. The ashes of Lent, the corpus on the crucifix,; the *memento mori*—all made life the good fight of St. Paul.[124]

So, with Yeats, let us swear that we hear the King's great horn. If all men must be soldiers; if life is conflict; if each day is a battle; if war is the father of all; if He came to bring not peace but a sword; if Catholicism is about swords, then all men must learn strategy, the *strategos*, merely everyman as soldier, remembering Roland at Roncesvalles, the Leper King at Montgisard, the Bruce at Blar Allt a Bhonnaich, the Bonnie Prince at Glennfinnan raising the tandem triumphans standard, Stonewall at Bull Run, Chamberlain at Gettysburg, Lee in the Wilderness, Churchill in London, MacArthur on Bataan, Lech Walesa in a Polish shipyard, Boris Yeltsin on a tank, the students at Tiananmen Square or in the streets of Tehran, who, shuddering with an iron taste in the mouth, fearing shame and defeat, on the brink of tears, skin stippling with terror, stands, is visible, maneuvers, feints, retreats, goes forward again, then makes a stand and plants the flag, the gorgeously emblazoned pennons flapping in the breeze, cries out like thunder "to the King, to the King, rally to the King" and tries to rally all disheartened wavering men to stand with him, shoulder to shoulder, in knightly solidarity, born as we all are, as was Christ, as was Jupiter-Zeus, as was the Leper King and the Bruce, as was William the Bastard, who became the Conqueror, the great Norman King, with backs against the wall.

PART TWO

MEMORY MAKER

Memory Maker

The Story of a Young Man's Death by Cancer

The grass was very tall where he was standing, so he took a step up onto smoother ground. From there he could see the lake, which stretched out green and smooth before him. A flock of white birds flew over, casting the ground in shadows, so that for a moment he felt a chill. But both the birds and the feeling passed. As he looked out over the waters there arose from the lake, where it had been entirely submerged, a great black bull that with stiff, strong steps came ashore, where it began to graze. The great bulk of its slate-black hide glistened with the waters and its horns—horns wide, thick, triangular-shone with the reflected colors of a sky now filled with sunset.

"Marcus . . . Marcus get up! It's seven-twenty."

Marcus turned over to glance at the clock. "Five more minutes," he thought, "five more minutes." This was not going to be a good day. It was probably going to be worse than yesterday.

"MARCUS GET UP!" Now his father's voice, instead of his Mom's, was loudly thundering, and his father's voice meant get up and get up NOW.

"I'm up. I'm up," hollered Marcus and trudged to the bathroom.

Through all his getting ready—the shower, the brushing teeth, the brushing hair, the brushing hair again and wondering how it'd look with the sides shaved, the hunting of blue jeans—Marcus was thinking about what was very likely going to happen after second period. What was very likely going to happen after second period was that Marcus was going to get his lights punched out if he didn't fork over three bucks.

Yesterday, two juniors whom he didn't know, though he'd seen them around, said they were going to kick his ass if he didn't have the three dollars today, and Marcus had the very funny feeling that this was not likely to be payment-in-full. Whether he paid or not, those guys were going to be hassling him everyday now.

And he heard that one of them had bit somebody's ear off at school last year and outside of school—well, he just hoped neither one of them knew where he lived.

"Marcus, come on now, I'm leaving," said his Dad. By the time Marcus got out to the car, his Dad was already in a bad mood. But he didn't say anything like he would have last year. In fact, Marcus' father didn't say much of anything to him anymore, except to ask him if he was feeling OK, or what the doctor had said. A lot had changed since Marcus got sick.

That had been a terrible day last year when they had gone to the doctor about that lump in his back. His father had been the first to notice it.

"Sheri, what's this?" he had said as he was hugging Marcus.

"What?" said Marcus's Mom.

"Come here. This," said his Dad.

When his Mom felt the lump, which, of course, Marcus had already noticed but hadn't said anything about, he saw his Mom and Dad exchange a look that meant something worse than they were going to say.

"What is it?" said Marcus, a quiver of mad mixing with fear in his voice.

"Oh, nothing. It's just a lump," said his Dad. "Nothing to worry about, but your Mom is going to make an appointment with the doctor."

This was bad news as far as Marcus was concerned, but since doctor's appointments usually were at least a few days away from the time you made one, Marcus pulled down this shirt and went back to watching TV.

"Why don't you call now," said his Dad, and he could already hear his mother dialing. Her voice was low and hushed on the phone. Marcus knew she didn't want him to hear her.

"The doctor says it's probably nothing to worry about, but he said we ought to go ahead and come in and let him look at it."

"I'll pull the car out," said his father.

"You mean we're going now?" said Marcus.

"Come on, Marcus," said his Mom, in a tone of voice he heard only one other time, when the roof caught on fire at their old house and she had told him to get out now.

The drive to the doctor had been a real trip, with about the fakiest conversation he had ever heard. His Dad had managed to ask him three questions without one of them being whether he was going to play any sports next year when he was a freshman. And his mother hadn't felt the need to say how sensitive he was. It was hard for Marcus and his parents to be anywhere, anytime together for very long without sports or being sensitive coming up.

But fakey had been better than scary, and what happened at the doctor's and at the hospital the next day had been scary, real scary; scarier, though Marcus didn't like to admit it, than anything that ever happened to him before. The doctor had been very business-like, had done a lot of tests, and then the next day they had checked into the hospital for a biopsy, which the doctor had said wouldn't hurt much, but it had hurt and he'd been sore. And Marcus had swallowed hard, trying not to cry when the doctor said the next day that the test had come back positive and he'd swallowed even harder when his father had said, "But what does that mean exactly?" And the doctor had said, "It means that Marcus has cancer," and even though he tried not to cry, he did, but only later on during the night when his mother was asleep on the cot next to his hospital bed; and he cried very quietly. He'd made no noise but knew his mother had felt the tears when she'd gotten up, thinking he was asleep and touched him.

Nothing since had been as bad as that night, though there'd been a lot of bad stuff, like the day the doctor said surgery wouldn't be possible, and then radiation, and now with school just getting started they were talking about the start of chemotherapy and how sick it might make him. "Too bad," he thought, "the chemotherapy couldn't start today, like right after second period."

Second period came very slowly that day, though the ride to school had gone way too fast. No, actually it had all gone very fast. It was just that Marcus seemed to suffer every second, feeling queasy and thinking about those guys, but every time he looked at his watch at least ten minutes had passed. One time he knew it could only have been five minutes, but his watch said fifteen. Marcus had suffered through first period history even more than usual since the teacher was not only boring, but she was also mean and always quick to jump on Marcus during those first few days for his doodling. For the whole first week of school, she seemed to take special pleasure in waiting until he had finished a whole picture and then jumping on him, tearing out the page and crumbling it up with a sneer.

"You're never going to amount to anything. All those pictures are is trash. Don't you do anything but read comics?" During the first week Marcus had thought about telling her he had cancer so maybe she would cut him some slack, but his father had absolutely insisted that he tell no one. There had been a big argument about this, since his mother thought it was wrong to keep it a secret. "What good does it do?" she had shouted one night at Marcus' father, who had angrily left the room. And then quietly, under her breath, without realizing that Marcus could overhear, "He's not afraid to admit it, Baby; you are."

Marcus had kept to what his father wanted the first two weeks of school. And it had slacked off from the teacher, probably because starting the second week she spent most of her time either sitting at her desk or out in the hall talking to some other teacher. But today he might be forced to tell someone, specifically those two A-holes after second period. Maybe they'd be afraid to touch a kid with cancer.

The day passed, however, without the two A-holes showing up. This left Marcus with three more dollars than he had planned on having. So after school, he stopped at the fantasy shop and bought a poster. That night he fell asleep after copying the poster in his sketchbook. He didn't wake up so many times like the night before.

Nothing much eventful happened for the new few weeks. Marcus gradually adjusted to life as a freshman in a large urban high school, which meant life as something a littler better than a worm, except a worm doesn't feel superior to 7th and 8th graders, which certainly he did. He even made a few friends. Not friends exactly—more like a few guys and one girl whom he hung out with before school and who all ate lunch together. It was a group formed by those who really didn't belong to a group and who's only shared concern was the need to avoid total isolation. Misfits you might call them. There was one guy named Shawn, a white kid, with buck teeth. Shawn was into ham radios and liked to listen to the BBC all the time. Sometimes at lunch when no one knew what else to say, Shawn would talk about what he had heard the night before on the BBC. Marcus didn't mind listening to stuff about the BBC so long as Shawn didn't mind listening to the latest about Stan Lee and Marvel Comics. Once or twice they even skipped last period together and walked over to the fantasy

store. By the second trip, though, Shawn was already bored and waiting at the door before Marcus had even finished going through the
first used-comics box, so Marcus didn't ask him again.

It wasn't much of a loss, however, because Marcus was soon
missing school again for his treatments. This time it was chemo
or "combined modality therapy," which is what his mother said
the book called it. There had been a big fight about this too, at
home, with his Mom arguing that they simply ought to tell the
school what was happening so that maybe they could schedule his
classes around it, and with his father insisting that no one needed
to know and that this was a family matter and that they would
handle it themselves.

What Marcus' mother was hoping is that maybe the school would
have a counselor who could talk to Marcus about what he was going
through and maybe talk to her and his father, too, since his father
refused to have anything to do with the hospital social worker whom
he didn't trust from day one—what does she know about what he's
going through?— and to whom he didn't want either Marcus or his
mother talking either.

Marcus' father won the fight by saying that if they knew at school,
word would get out and the kids would isolate him, which was the
last thing, of course, that his mother wanted, and she was used to going along with his father anyway.

Throughout the whole discussion, Marcus had said only that he
didn't want to miss lunch. So in the end it was decided to schedule
his treatments first thing every morning since his mother didn't go to
work until noon and Marcus had study hall first period.

Once the treatments started, however, it became very clear, very
quickly that his plan wasn't going to work, because the 'getting
zapped,' as Marcus called it, took far too much a toll on him, leav-

ing him feeling tired, weary, drained, and eventually as sick as sick could be.

So the plan was altered, with Marcus' mother talking to the school, explaining the situation, and working out a home-school program, so that Marcus, as his father said, would not fall too far behind with his school work.

The days soon fell into a regular routine. Marcus would get up with his parents in the morning and watch cartoons while they were getting dressed. Then, after his father left for work, he and his mother would drive to the hospital, where he would get zapped. When the treatments had first started last spring, he thought the initial testing had been worse—all that getting poked and prodded, stuck and stabbed, the x-rays, scans, blood tests, and the laxative that they gave him really cleaned him out good. More had come out than he thought had ever gone in.

By the second week, however, Marcus had changed his mind. The chemo was worse.

On the way home, he and his mother would talk, but he and his mother had always talked a lot, so that was nothing new. For the first few days, he would talk his mother into stopping at Grandy's where he really liked the biscuits with extra gravy. Pretty soon, though, it was his mother talking him into stopping because Marcus wasn't feeling much like eating. But they would stop even if it meant that when his mother got home from work later that evening she would find the biscuits and gravy cold on the kitchen table.

From Grandy's they went by school where he would go in to get his work for the day. His father had insisted that he do this, so as his father said—his father always had something to say about school— he wouldn't get behind. Pretty soon it was Marcus' mother going in to get the work and pretty soon his mother would find it too on the kitchen table when she got home. It wasn't cold like the biscuits, but it was untouched.

In the afternoon, he was alone. Despite everything, he liked it. Again and again, he sorted through his comics collection, tallying up the value. And when he got tired of that, he would take up his sketchbook and begin to draw, covering sheet after sheet with grotesque and curious shapes, each with a story to tell and dialogue to express, all of which he would pencil in; and then Marcus would add the colors—colors warm and deep and tangible like the comics that he read. Colors almost warm to the touch and deep enough for the eye to swim in. He even invented his own superhero, like Black Lightening from the seventies.

Occasionally he'd go look in the refrigerator whose shelves were fast accumulating every treat known to man. Most of the time he would just look and close the door.

His Dad got home first. "Say, Marcus, how are you doing? How did it go today? Did you see the doctor?" his Dad would be asking him, as he headed back for the bedroom, where he'd empty his pockets on the large dresser, which used to be one of Marcus' main sources for extra comic money, and then change into his tennis shoes and shorts, and then he would be out to the back with a basketball, with Marcus, at least during the first few weeks, right behind him.

His Dad was an incredible basketball player. He had played in college and before he had got hurt had at least a long shot at the NBA. But he had gotten hurt, which Marcus had heard his mother say, might not have been such a bad thing since it was then that his Dad had settled down, hit the books, and become what his father said was one "pretty damn good attorney." But his father sure could play.

Bop, bop, bop, and then the Move, the arc and the swish. His Dad would run and gun, shoot and swish until to Marcus he seemed to be nothing but pure grace in motion. Bop, bop, bop, bop, bop, bop, and then that long cool quiet, with man and ball in air, and then the DUNK, which made his father seem ten feet tall in the eyes of his son.

After Marcus got cancer, his father didn't every third shot pop the ball to him, which was the signal to begin the nightly pick-up game at which Marcus wasn't very good and whose end always left them a little angry with each other. Now, he was allowed to sit on the porch and watch, which was entirely alright with him.

His Dad would play until his mother had gotten home and gotten dinner ready. He would sit with them and sooner or later "eat something" and then a little more to keep them from fighting.

The fight wouldn't exactly happen at the dinner table. It would happen, in hushed tones, when his Father would accuse his mother of not doing enough and she would accuse him of not talking enough. And then there would be the "what's there to talk about argument," which was an old one in his house.

In the old days Marcus would be required to do his homework, have it checked, and then maybe an hour or two of TV, with his parents very careful to keep an eye on what he was watching.

These days, that too was different. Retreating into their bedroom not long after dinner, they would leave Marcus in the living room with free run of the cable. Flipping back and forth, he did take in a little of the great forbidden, taboo MTV, but soon he was back with his cartoons and his Saturday Night Live reruns.

One night he called up Shawn. "Hey man, this is Marcus. What's happening?"

Shawn had filled him in about school, especially the big event of the fall: the killing of two guys in a shooting. "Are you doing OK, Marcus? Everyone says you're sick."

"Oh, I'm OK, man. Nothing's wrong. I gotta just, you know, stay out for awhile."

"When are you coming back to school?"

"I don't know," said Marcus. "Soon."

Marcus was at the lake again.

But it wasn't evening anymore. Instead, it seemed like the late afternoon, the hottest part, when everything is still and lifeless, except the flies whose endless buzz filled his head as they whirred and sucked at the lake mud.

Out of the corner of his eye Marcus saw a long, colorless snake slither down, down to the water's edge, flare its head and then begin to lap at the water.

And out of the corner of his eye, Marcus saw something else.

With his eyes filmed by the heat and the glare from the surface of the lake, Marcus couldn't be sure. Was it something? But then he began to focus, and as he did, he sucked his breath and froze, stuck to the spot. There was something there. No, not something, *someone*. There was someone standing there at the edge of the lake. It was a low, squat, barely visible figure. Marcus strained to see. "Good Lord, it's a man!" Marcus gasped and as he gasped the figure took one quick step into the light.

Now, still frozen, Marcus really sucked his breath because standing not ten yards away was something like he'd drawn, but not something like he'd ever seen before. It looked like a superhero from the planet, well, not the planet Earth. This guy was something. He wasn't a giant or anything. In fact, he was about the same height as Marcus, who had always been very tall for his age, which was why his Dad was always trying to push him into basketball. No, he wasn't very tall, but God he was wide. He was broad. He was built—built like Thor or Conan. But he wasn't white, he was black, jet black, coal black, like polished ebony, like the shadow of a great, broad river on a moonless night. His skin glistened. His chest and arms were massive and he had a great round belly that sat atop two legs as thick as tree trunks. His neck was as big as Marcus' thighs, and around his neck, shoulders, and wrists were ornaments of gold. What little covering he wore was red. His hair was greased and knotted, and atop his head he wore two great horns out from under which there glared two powerful, dark eyes. And they were looking straight at Marcus.

"Geeze, he would be fun to draw," thought Marcus, in the instant between his being surprised and his being totally petrified, as the guy suddenly sprang toward him.

The guy covered the ground a lot faster then he was supposed to, or a lot faster than Marcus was used to people covering ground, and at the end of this very fast covering of ground, he jumped up, spun in the air and came down with a hard elbow straight and deep into Marcus' chest.

"Aaahhh," said Marcus, as he sat down hard with a now-very-sore behind and a chest that would soon be sore as soon as it stopped being numb and Marcus got his breath back.

"Aaaaahhhhh," said Marcus with his eyes about to jump out of his head.

"AAAAAHHHHH," said Marcus, getting his breath back and now, though still seated, scrambling backwards, scraping his behind with heels and palms clawing, clawing the earth and pushing backwards as fast as he could go.

With the same amount of energy that the guy had covered the ten yards, Marcus got about two feet away, but at the end of this burst of speed there was not going to be any flashy, wrestling move. Instead there would be what there always was from Marcus when he found himself in a sticky situation: some very fast talk.

And it had to be fast because this guy looked very much like he was about to pile-drive Marcus three feet into the earth.

"Wait. Wait. Wait. What are you doing? What are you doing?" said Marcus. "Wait a minute. Wait a minute."

The guy paused, barely. But he still looked like a cat about to spring. No, not a cat, a Tiger.

"Wait a minute," said Marcus, pushing himself back another two feet for safekeeping.

"Who are you? What are you doing here? What am I doing here? What's going on?"

"I am Murani," boomed the figure, not glaring anymore but still looking very fierce and with every vein about to jump out of his muscles. "I'm here to teach you how to fight."

"How to fight?" Marcus' mouth hung wide open. "How to fight?"

"That's right," said the man, as he jumped up and came down like a hammer, pinning Marcus to the earth.

"Let me up! Let me up!" screamed Marcus, drenched with sweat and in a voice partly muffled by the two legs scissoring his head.

"I'll let you up when you're ready to fight," said the man.

"I can't fight," pleaded Marcus. "I'm not a fighter. I'm sick. I have cancer."

"All the more reason to learn how to fight," said the man, tightening his scissor-hold so that Marcus could hardly breath.

Now at about this point, Marcus was fast getting over his "I can't believe this is happening" feeling and was starting to believe that this was happening and that he'd better do something real quick. His change in attitude probably had something to do with the fact that he was choking. So he doubled up his fist, aimed directly for the groin and sailed in the hardest punch of his life. In fact, it was the only punch of his life.

"Better," said the man without even flinching, but loosening his hold a bit so that Marcus could wiggle out and scramble to his feet.

"Who the hell are you?" demanded Marcus, now pumped up and angry and ready to hit again and again and again, if that's what it took.

The Murani rolled over on his back, put his arms behind his head, and smiled.

"I told you my name. And I told you why I've come. I'm here to teach you how to fight. I came against you. You came against me. That's good."

"Came against me. Came against me," Marcus sputtered. "You attacked me, that's what you did you son of a . . . " Marcus almost finished before landing *oomph*, flat on his back, courtesy of a darting, quick move by Murani, who then began to laugh.

Through the weeks that followed, Marcus did begin to fight. His days were filled with feats of courage. It's hard to have cancer and not develop courage, even if you didn't have it before, because you have to fight, you have to fight constantly at home and at the hospital, with nurses and doctors, with parents, too, and with your own body, your own heart, your own soul, your own pain. Your body will hurt. Your strength will go. Your hair will fall out. Your fears will rise up and stalk you in the night.

Fortunately, Marcus had the Murani, who in the beginning would only walk with him in his dreams, but soon he would overtake him in the daylight hours as well, appearing in Marcus' waking thoughts and fantasies and dreams and even in his sketchbook, where one morning Marcus found the dark eyes and dark features staring at him in what had been intended as a portrait of the friendly lab tech who had come to take some blood once.

One day as they were wrestling, with Marcus' back caked with sweat and dust from being thrown to the ground again and again, the Murani began to talk, telling him a story.

> Once there was a great King. Mzilikazi was his name. And this great King had need of a new recruit to join his bodyguard. So he sent his chieftain into the countryside to find one.
>
> Some weeks later, the chieftain returned. With him stood a young man, tall, well-formed and hard-muscled.
>
> "Tell me the story of his finding," said the King.
>
> "Many days I searched," said his chieftain, "with little luck until I chanced upon a crowd. At the center of the crowd two boys were fighting. Five times this boy knocked the other down. Each blow was like a lion's charge."
>
> "How did it end?" said the King.
>
> "I stopped it," said the chieftain. "Another blow and the other boy would have been killed."
>
> "You have chosen badly," said old Mzilikazi. "Bring me the other boy."
>
> "But why?" said the chieftain. "This boy is a fighter."
>
> "We can teach anyone to fight," said the King.
>
> "What we cannot teach is how never to surrender."

The wind whistled off the plain.

"When your heart is frail," said Murani, looking off into the distance where the hills rose to meet the clouds in a milky blue light, "think upon this story. Your heart will feel it and grow strong."

Not long after, the treatments stopped, with the doctor explaining that while the results, so far, had been somewhat encouraging, the body could only take so much before needing to stop for awhile to re-new its resources. The doctor said all this while addressing everyone but looking at no one in particular. But as he talked, Marcus' mother reached across and took his father's hand.

Three people walked out of the hospital that day feeling better than they'd felt in months. They needed something to hang on to. Some shred of hope, some beam of light. Marcus' parents were still holding hands as they walked to the car and Marcus too had a bit of a spring to his step.

As soon as they were on the road, Marcus asked if they could roll down the windows. The wind across his face felt good. His nose felt cleared at last of the hospital smell, of the Pine-Sol scent, the gasoline of the parking lot, the heavy smell of the women's perfume as he walked past the admission's office on his way to the treatment center.

Yes, the wind felt good and as it swept across his face he thought he caught just a touch of a fresh-bread smell floating over perhaps from the big bread factory that they passed each day on the way to the hospital.

"How about some biscuits?" Marcus chimed from the back seat. "How about some lunch?"

The words were hardly out of his mouth before his Dad was pull-ing off the highway and heading straight towards Grandy's, where Marcus downed a good half-dozen biscuits swimming thick with but-ter and gravy.

On the way out, sucking on a toothpick, he breathed that air again, took it down good and deep so that he even stretched his toes.

Marcus wasn't through with the hospital. Much more often than he would have liked, he found himself sitting in the large, spacious lobby, which felt more like a mall than a waiting room, listening to the fountain and watching the woman go from plant to plant sprinkling each with water. As she felt the soil for moisture, while looking up at no one in particular, Marcus would sometimes catch her eye and smile and she would smile back. There were still tests. His "progress was being closely monitored," as he had learned to say.

It was not only the doctors who were monitoring his progress. Every couple of days Marcus would hear his Dad say to his Mom something like, "I think he's doing a lot better. I think he's gaining back the weight. I'm feeling real encouraged about the whole thing now." To which his mother would respond, "Well, he's certainly feeling better."

And Marcus was feeling better and was putting back on a little weight. More than once he had sampled some of the goodies that had piled up in the refrigerator. He was drawing a lot more too now and even tried school a couple of half days, with a baseball cap to cover up his baldness. No one paid much attention to him, except for Shawn who even came over to his house once or twice. To Marcus' great dismay Shawn turned out to be a pretty good basketball player with a pretty good jump shot. His father liked that.

With things going so well, the tests had been reduced in Marcus' mind to a necessary bother, which he didn't think much about until that day when his father came home in the middle of the day to go with him and his mother to meet with the doctor.

"Come in, please," said the doctor, opening the door for him and his parents to come in. Before, the doctor was never there before they got there. They always had to wait on him.

"I'm afraid the news isn't so good this morning," he said in a voice that seemed to come from a long way off. "The cancer is spreading. There are a number of things we're still going to try, and we'll try to make everything as comfortable as possible. There's no reason to give up hope. But it is serious."

Marcus' mother gripped her hands and began to cry.

The rest of the day went by rather quickly for Marcus. He did as he would normally do, spending the afternoon and early evening watching TV, with his parents watching it with him a little bit, but getting up and going into the other room to do things, but then coming back. They all ate dinner in front of the TV that night, watching an old rerun of Saturday Night Live. It was the one with Mr. Rambo's Neighborhood. It felt good to laugh a little.

After dinner, Marcus went in to take a bath, staying in the water a long, long time, studying his body, the frailness of it, the bruises on his arms from the constant blood tests and injections. His legs looked so skinny to him. He could feel his ribs. After the bath, he splashed on some of his father's cologne, then went on to bed after kissing his Mother and Dad goodnight.

He lay there in the dark for a long, long while, watching on his door the pale silver glow and flickering shadows of his parents' TV. After the news, he heard the TV go off and the house fell dark and very silent, with the only light being that from the bathroom in the hall. Then that too was blocked out for a second as he felt someone in the room. It was Marcus' father who stood at the foot of the bed looking at Marcus. Neither stirred for a moment, then he felt his father go around to the other side of the bed, pull back the cover and slide in. In a little while, they both fell asleep.

As together that night they sat in the glow and warmth of a great brush and timber fire that it had taken them nearly an hour to build, the Murani's voice began to sound melodious and clear in what Marcus could only figure was some kind of ancient song—about what he had no idea, though certain rhythms and sounds seemed somehow familiar.

In the clear meadow the light from the fire seemed to spread out endlessly, mixing with the moonlight and the incredibly bright stars, so that the place in which they sat could hardly have been brighter.

Murani's hair was oiled and he wore a red cloth about him. His eyes seemed alive and quivering and dark and bright like two dark fishes glimpsed hovering far, far beneath the deepest parts of the clear green lake water.

The voice trailed off, ebbing with the flame which now began to crackle, spraying the air with orange, yellow embers.

"Make me a memory," said Murani.

"A memory?" blurted Marcus, who had almost fallen asleep.

"Yes, a memory. I was told you are a memory maker, Marcus. You're certainly not a wrestler," said Murani, with, what was for Marcus, a little too broad of a smile.

"No. No. No way. I'm not a memory whatever you call it. A memory maker. I don't even know what you're talking about." But something in him had leapt up at the word. He couldn't help it. And he couldn't help but notice that this was the first time that Murani had actually spoken to him by name.

"Are you a poet?" continued Murani, paying as little attention to Marcus as he often did on the wrestling field when Marcus was trying to explain what he had meant to do.

"Are you a poet? Can you bring the dawn up from the dust? Can you bring it up through the soles of a man's feet so that his thighs and spine begin to tingle and his heart sees with the joy of the first morning on the earth?"

"No," said Marcus.

"Are you a storyteller, then? Can you make the old ones walk upon the face of the earth again? Can you speak of lion killings and the slaying of the crocodile? Can you tell of cattle raids and kings? Can you tell of how the Lake stole water from the Sky and then of how the Sky made stars instead of fishes because a star no man can catch?"

"I'm none of those," said Marcus, afraid now that he would fail as he had failed too many times for one life already.

"What are you then?" said Murani. "Make me a memory," fixing on him with eyes as friendly but as faceless as a summer evening full of stars.

A long silence held him in its thrall.

"Well," said Marcus. "I guess I could draw," hoping somehow that he had said the right thing. "But there's nothing to draw with."

Murani handed him the sharpened stick on which he had been carving as he sang.

"What good is this?" said Marcus, now genuinely puzzled.

"Your stick will speak to the earth as my song has spoken to the wind, my friend. Let them speak. You with she will make my memory."

'This is crazy," thought Marcus. "This is crazy," said Marcus. "I can't draw anything here and besides if I were able to do something it will just rain tonight or the wind will blow it or somebody will . . . "

"No, my friend. The earth will remember. Someday I will return to the earth. And then I will remember, too."

Marcus began to draw. Bending down upon his knees and taking up the stick as he would a paintbrush, he began to draw. First, he drew the line of the lake and the tall long water grass waving in the wind. He put a stork up in the left-hand corner and then a long crocodile laying lethal in his mud pool. Down below there came a lion, proud, sinewy, and grave with a great mane and not an ounce of fat, and then as the lines began to thin and thicken there were Murani and him together, wrestling, laughing, squirting water from a waterskin. And as you looked at it you could feel the muscles rippling, the deepness of the laugh, and almost taste the coolness of the water as it arched its sweet, cool, glittering track into the warm hard ground. And then he scraped out half a dozen embers from the fire so as to fill the sky with burning stars and then he scraped out more to put a fire in the center, with him and Murani sleeping by it on a soft, downy antelope skin.

Suddenly the spell broke, he awakened from his trance and glanced back behind him to see the Murani crouching over him, whistling with pleasure, his eyes and face aglow, and the great bulk of his neck like a boulder from the side of which the moon was shining.

"Good," he said. "It is good." Then he stood up to his full height and stretched, blocking out the stars.

"One treasure for another," he said, and below the drawing he laid down his spear.

"I see you Memory Maker. Glory of the People." And then he turned on his heel and with slow, proud steps walked off into the night.

Marcus waited for what seemed like a long, long time for Murani to return. Sitting cross-legged in the dark, he fixed his gaze into the fire, waiting to hear the sound of those familiar footsteps that fell the way an ancient tree lays down its evening shadow. But only the soft rustle of the night breeze filled his ears.

After what seemed an even longer time, Marcus scrambled up, with his legs a little stiff from sitting, and turned around to look through the tall grass towards the lake whose surface sparkled smooth and still with the moonlight. Hearing nothing and now seeing nothing: no sign of movement, no trunk-like silhouette against the water's edge, he walked out five paces, then ten, then all the way to the water.

"Murani," he whispered. "Murani, not now, not now." And then louder, "Murani, where are you?" And then, finally shouting, his voice beginning to quiver with, first, doubt and finally desperation. "Murani, Murani, don't leave me. Not now." But still no sound, no sound at all, and then he felt wild eyes upon his back and then the tell-tale sound of a crocodile sliding from the muck into the water.

With that, he spun around to look for the fire whose flame, though growing smaller now, continued to burn golden.

"At least that's still there," thought Marcus, trying to talk himself into believing that what was happening wasn't happening. Over the last few months he'd gotten fairly good at that. "He's probably just circled round and beat me back. He'll be there grinning and laughing all ready to tell me what I should have done instead of what I did."

But when Marcus cleared the edge of the tall grass from where he could see the fire, it wasn't one person who sat at the fire; instead, it was three around it with something or someone else sitting at the very edge of the firelight, so that you couldn't really see him.

Careful now not to make any noise, setting each foot down as noiselessly as he could, Marcus approached the circle but pulled up short while still concealed by darkness.

What he saw were three figures, three shadows, three faces illumined in the dark, three pairs of eyes glowing like embers fanned by a breath.

"Seat yourself, boy," hissed a voice in his ear.

When Marcus jumped and started to turn a cold hand gripped his shoulder. "Do not look at me, boy. It will go the worse for you," the voice hissed again. Marcus' skin turned cold and clammy.

"Do as you are told. Seat yourself with the others."

Marcus did as he was told exactly, crouching down in front of the fire about as quick as he could go.

"No, exactly like the other," said the voice.

This Marcus did as well, crossing his legs and sitting where in what was now the fourth corner of an almost perfect square.

Since he was looking directly into the fire and had just come from the dark, it took an instant for his eyes to focus, but when they did what he saw was three other young men, about the same age as himself. Two were black, tough-looking, hard and muscular. One wore a red bandana over his head. Both had earrings and the one with the red bandana, he may have had a scar. The other boy was white, frail, and thin, like Marcus. But he didn't look scared. He certainly didn't look as scared as Marcus felt.

"North. South. East. West," said the voice, a little louder now, but even more chilling, more menacing, chanting, drumming, coming inside the circle of the fire so that Marcus could see him better, could see the cloak and hood of feathers, the feathers shimmering, shining, each feather a tiny dancing flame.

"North. South. East. West."

With about the last "North, South, East and West," Marcus had given up all hope that this guy was Murani dressed up to teach a new lesson. No, this was different, truly different.

The figure continued to circle the boys like a bird of prey. No, thought Marcus, glumly, more like a vulture.

And then this. He leapt up high over the boys' heads and landed in the middle of the circle where the fire had been but where he now was, a face burning in the flame, a flame that had become a face.

"You cross now. You cross now," he cackled. "The hunt. The hunt," and then the quiet and then the voice again, "For you the lion," and the flame leapt out and seemed to play about the features of the guy with the bandana and then where he was sitting, nothing, nothing, but the darkest air. "For you the crocodile." Again the flame leapt out to touch the other boy and they were all boys now, trembling and quaking. "For you the boar," the flame leapt out but this time it seemed to take the form of a long arm, a long spear of light that nicked the white boy on the forehead and then he too was gone. "For you. For you, the greatest of beasts, the greatest of Warriors. For you the buffalo." Again, the flame leapt out and Marcus, suddenly in the space where there should have been a heartbeat, was standing naked in the shallows of the lake, with the cool lake water swirling around his ankles. He was holding a spear. His hair was oiled and shining. His eyes burned with the color of the lion's coat when the lion walks in the heat of the African Sun.

Rising out of the waters the young man came silently ashore and into the tall grass where the great black beast was waiting. "I see you, Great One," said the Warrior, and stared into the eyes of the slate-black bull, eyes that raged red, dark, earth-red, core-red, red like the color of lava, like the color of earth when it throws up its most ancient, living flames. The bull stood trembling, pawing at the dust, with white, mud-caked, dust-caked hooves biting, chopping at the ground. "I see you Great One," said the Warrior, and lifted up his spear, high, high, so that it seemed to move among the stars and then it flew, flew like the wind at the bull as it began its charge, the air hot and heavy, the great, rank smell, the smell of all that is, of all that was, of all that has ever been living, filling the Warrior's nostrils, filling up his heart, and then he felt it, the great long horns singing in his belly, singing in his heart, lifting him up higher and higher, tossing him in the air, around and around and around, trying to shake out the spear, shake off the Warrior impaled on his horns, shake off the fear, the cold, cold fear now filling up his heart. Down. Down, down went the Warrior, into the heart of the bull, into the heart of the Warrior, into the heart of the evening, into the heart of the earth.

All now grew very still.

A coffee pot sat in the middle of the kitchen table. There was barely room for it because of all the cakes and pies and hams everywhere.
"What's all this food doing here?" wondered Marcus. "Mamma, Papa,
what are you doing?" but Marcus' folks didn't seem to hear him.

They were sitting there at the table, drinking coffee. Both were
dressed in their Sunday best. Each sipped from their coffee. His
mother had been crying. "Mamma. Papa. What's wrong?" Still, they
didn't hear him. In fact, they didn't seem to notice him at all.

"I think I'm going to take a few weeks off," said his mother. "I
need the time. I've still got a lot to take care of. You know it really was
nice. I didn't expect so many people. Even Mrs. Dickey was there.
She was always good to Marcus. I think the fourth grade was his best
year. You know she told me she kept his picture."

His father said nothing.

"Baby," said his mother leaning over to softly brush the top of his
father's hand. "He's gone. You've got to accept that."

His father jerked away, pulling away even harder when his mother
reached for him again.

"Alright," she said, sitting back deep in her chair, crossing her arms
and then beginning to tremble, softly, silently, alone, all to herself.

"You know what's wrong, Baby. You're mad at him for leaving
you." The words were no more out of her mouth when she began to
cry. His father jumped up hard, knocking over his coffee, staring at it
and then going quickly outdoors, where he tossed away his coat and
tie, rolled up his sleeves and grabbed up the basketball.

Marcus was on the porch now, as he had often been, watching
his Dad move with the same old graceful motion. There was not
much dribbling now, only moves and spiraling through the air, slip-

ping as he came down on his good shoes, but then in the air again, again, and again, and again the swish, swish, swish, hard, quick, mechanical now, not like a kite but like a piston, hard, drilling, drilling, hard, down into the throat, to the neck, into the throat of everything that would stand against him, going for the hole, for the hole, for the hole, and then his father stopped, stopped like an engine turning off. Soaked with sweat, the veins and muscles bulging through his shirt, he had sat down right where he stood and stared off into nothing.

"I'm sorry, Papa," said Marcus, but his voice blended with the warm dusk breeze, which blew up now, carrying on it a hint of honeysuckle.

He died on April 3, just as the air was turning into springtime. Nearly the whole school turned out for his funeral. Of course, for a lot of kids, it was just an excuse to get out of school. But for probably more than Marcus could have ever believed, it was a gesture of affection for a kid who never hurt anybody and who could draw a cartoon that would light up anybody's day. Shawn skipped school that day, so he could go by the fantasy store and spend five bucks on a comic. He stayed a little longer at the cemetery than anyone else, so he could lay the comic on the graveside. "OK, it was kind of stupid," he thought. "But what the hell."

A little later that evening, his mother had gone into his room to sit for a little while and to get some of his things together. She was in no hurry, but it didn't make sense to leave everything the way it was.

"Baby, come in here," she said after being in there barely for a moment.

"What?" said Marcus' father.

"Come in here, please," she was nearly begging.

So his father walked slowly into the room, as if he were afraid that something in there might hurt him.

"What?" he said, with his eyes meeting hers and then following hers to the nightstand next to Marcus' bed. And there his eyes fell upon a drawing so life-like and so beautiful that you almost believed the figures were in motion. There on the sheet was a drawing of Marcus' father, dressed in the blue and gold of his college career, leaping high to the basket with the ball poised so gracefully on his fingertips that it seemed an extension of his arm and his arm an extension of the air and indeed Marcus' father did seem to be all air, all leaping, floating; he seemed to be suspended motionless just like the stars which floated above him in a vivid dark night air, and there was Marcus, small, seated at the side of the driveway with his sketchbook in his lap, drawing with a pen, an old-timey feathery-type pen, a pen that looked much like a flashing spear or a warrior's arrow. The colors were so bright and bold, so beautiful and real, that it took your breath away, which is what Marcus' father did, he caught his breath, and stared in wide and breathless wonder at the picture. It bore the title, scribbled in low and lovingly, ME AND MY DAD.

And then Marcus' father sat down on the edge of the bed and began to cry.

Softly, Marcus' mother backed out of the room and gently closed the door.

Outside it began to rain.

PART THREE

TOWARD AN HONOR PSYCHOLOGY

Honor and majesty are before Him;
Strength and beauty are in His sanctuary.

—Psalm 96:6

What Do I Do as a Counselor?

> I believe that man will not merely endure: he will prevail. He is immortal, not because he alone among creatures has an inexhaustible voice, but because he has a soul, a spirit capable of compassion and sacrifice and endurance.
>
> —William Faulkner, Nobel Prize Speech

What do I do as a counselor? Let me start by referring you to William Faulkner's Nobel Prize-winning acceptance speech because the language borrows heavily from him, from the magnificence of that speech, and from the magnificence of the vision and tradition out of which it sprang.

I try to be prop and pillar, a model and support, if you like, for that would be the way we counselors might put it, but prop and pillar . . .

I try to be considerate, to show consideration in all things, which means empathy, which means the golden rule, which means sensitivity, and trying to put myself in other people's shoes, what my friend, James Gritter, calls hospitality. I try to be compassionate, understanding and a comfort.

I try to honor people—I like to refer to what I do as "honor psychology." By honoring I mean identifying, acknowledging, crediting, admiring, praising a client's suffering, virtues, courage, endurance, wisdom, ideals, burdens, triumphs, achievements, excellences; I try to honor the grandeur and greatness of their souls, their spirits, their lives, their histories, their cultures; I try to speak and think on these things, focus on them, recall them, reminisce, commemorate, amplify, extend, in a way that restores some continuities in their lives, some depth, some connection to their families, histories, cultures,

language, faith, tradition. I try by word and gesture and emphasis and
metaphor and story and information to connect them with the best
in their traditions in solidarity with the best in all traditions.

By honoring them in this way I try to foster their laying claim to
what Faulkner called "the old verities": compassion, courage, common sense, pity, pride, honor, love. Eliot called them "the permanent
things"; Yeats, "the Presences that passion, piety or affection knows."

I try to help them lay this claim, extend it, build on it, to make it
fruitful and life-furthering, by strategizing, by giving solid, sound,
sensible advice, problem-solving, developing effective plans of action
that carry them towards these goals.

Strategizing, the foundation of successful problem-solving: what
is it? Strategic thinking in therapy is the envisaging of a client in
situation, with situation understood as a fluid, changing set of in-
dependent and interdependent but always interactive variables (the
fog of war in the parlance of military strategists), in such a way as
to organize and mobilize a client's strengths, resources and abilities, with realistic allowance for his limitations, to achieve his vital
interests through means that economize effort, that is, maximize
chances for success, while minimizing risk, loss, pain, damage, difficulty, hardship. At its worst, good strategy is economical. At its
best, it is elegant. "Easy does it" is not a bad motto. And it may take
a while.

By laying claim to these old verities, these "permanent things,"
and by building on them, I try to help my clients better endure and
prevail in the Battle of Life, for whatever else Life is, Life is surely
that: a Battle. As the Good Book says *"militia est vita hominii"*—"a
soldier's service is the life of man." In St. Paul's language, of which I
am sure Faulkner would approve, I want them to "run the race," to
"win the prize" to "put on the armor" and to always remember that

of all these things, though we speak with the tongues of angels, we have nothing if we have not love. These are my Southern roots.

In general, I practice a long term, open ended psychotherapy based on the premises that 1) although life has many good things about it, many satisfactions, it is often a struggle; 2) that we all essentially want the same things; and that 3) the goal is to endure and prevail with some measure of decency, fulfillment and self respect.

The role of the therapist is to model, that is, set a good example, support and empathize, to encourage by focusing on ideals and strengths, to speak an uplifting language, and to educate with ideas, information and coping strategies.

Calling my approach honor psychology gets to the heart of what I do; it represents an attempt to truly honor people in a manner that encourages them to lay claim to their honor, that is to say, to keep faith with the best about themselves—these verities and truths, these permanent things: love and honor, pity and pride, compassion and self-sacrifice. In this way my approach somewhat converges with some of the cutting edge developments in positive psychology while also recalling the inspiring ideals of existential writers. To keep faith with the best about ourselves ennobles human life—gives space and scope to what Abraham Lincoln called " the better angels of our nature." In a fundamental and existential sense, that is, in a way that resonates with a fully human meaning that takes into account our anxieties and imperfections, our "angst" as the existentialists say, the goal of honor psychology is to "get better."

The Course of Counseling

> Among those with a disposition toward caring and curing, some
> have brought inclinations and temperaments specially suited to
> the practice of psychological healing—a respectful and interested
> way of listening; a readily felt trustworthiness; a compassion-
> ate and sympathetic response to those who suffer; a capacity for
> arousing and sustaining hope; and a calm response to disturbing
> or frightening clinical states.
>
> —Stanley Jackson, *Care of the Psyche:*
> *A History of Psychological Healing*

The first step in honor therapy is the development of rapport. That
is, it will take a while for you to get to know and trust me and to
feel comfortable talking about your private feelings and concerns.
Trust between a client and professional is expected to grow slowly
and to be based on counseling's capacity to prove itself as useful and
worthwhile in helping with concrete problems and in addressing a
client's concerns.

As counseling develops the client can expect to:

Address loss: loss, trauma, grief, anxiety, suffering are major themes
in honor therapy. Often behind or contributing to depression, anxiety, irritability and bouts of anger, even near-manic and dis-associa-
tive experiences are profound, sometimes terrible and terrifying, but
nonetheless unacknowledged loss and trauma. Where a genetic pre-
disposition may exist to various kinds of disorders, loss and trauma
appear to sometimes trigger or exacerbate it. What can one do about
something like that? The answer is: we can identify those losses,
voice, grieve, and acknowledge them, do them justice in whatever

way we can through various kinds of observances. We can try to find comfort and learn how to comfort ourselves somewhat by finding meaning. We can also recognize how the grief and pain plays out through and affects ordinary daily living.

Ventilate: talk things out with an understanding and sympathetic listener. You may cry, rage, and unload some of the day's cares.

Learn to identify feelings: sometimes we suffer enormously with insomnia, stress, headaches, stomachaches, tension etc. because we are unable or unwilling to identify and express our feelings. Learn to say: "I'm sad, lonely, depressed, fearful, angry, or anxious." Often we "act out" our feelings, that is, we do something unhelpful or destructive that expresses them without our being aware of it.

Learn to identify patterns of behavior: sometimes we get into ruts, vicious circles, have destructive actions and reactions, so that we go on doing the same old things even when it doesn't work anymore or causes ourselves or someone else pain.

Develop insight: understanding ourselves, our relationships with others, our family, our past, with the world and with God is often the first step toward accepting ourselves.

Learn new coping and communication skills: sometimes we find ourselves blocked or unhappy simply because we can't think of a way to do or say it differently.

Manage crises or practical problems: counseling provides access to specific, step-by-step guidance on what to do and how to respond to life's dilemmas and conflicts.

Acquire parenting skills: there truly exists today "a war upon parents" that makes raising kids, especially when they become teenagers, sometimes feel like an impossible task. How to communicate with your child, how to understand their developmental needs and processes, and, often most critically, how to effectively discipline in a way based on encouragement and guidance rather than control are questions that counseling can answer.

Prioritize: the burdens, complexity and accelerated pace and hyper-stimulation of modern life can easily become so disorienting that we become confused, lose our focus, and forget who we really are and what we're striving for. Counseling can help with determining and setting new goals so that we are can better stay focused and keep our priorities straight.

Laying claim to honor and a sense of purpose: one of the distinguishing traits of honor therapy is its emphasis on honor, on human dignity and pride, and its view of human life as a struggle, as a Battle at times. The ultimate goal is truly to get better—better in the sense of feeling better, which means, of course, more peace and inner harmony, but there is also a moral imperative implicit in this phrase: the imperative to get better, to successfully meet the challenge of life, to rise to that challenge by laying claim and keeping faith with all that is best in us: our ideals and aspirations, our courage, compassion, our common sense, our personal and family honor, the honor of our communities, our Church,—even God's honor, if you will. Honor therapy is spiritual in that I believe that the best in us is ultimately our spirit and the theological virtues—Faith, Hope, and Charity. But I believe in the classical virtues, too—prudence, justice, fortitude, temperance; that is to say, honor therapy is existential in its belief in the need for spiritedness—what the Greeks called *thymos*—in the effort to endure and prevail in life, to survive, feel secure, succeed and finally find, true significance, in the sense of finding something worth standing and sacrificing for, even to the point of death. Isn't that the ultimate question for all of us: what do we really believe is worth dying for?

With children and teenagers the methods and goals of counseling are adapted to age-appropriate developmental needs and potential. For example, children usually respond best to play therapy, art therapy, and story telling, which are their primary means of communicating their feelings and issues. With adolescents, counseling may be more specifically focused on goal setting, accountability for one's actions and developing respect and the ability to negotiate with authority than it would be with adults. Counseling with children and adolescents always includes parenting support, encouragement and guidance.

Counseling can help in these ways and in others for yourself, your marriage, your children and family. To succeed, however, requires your commitment to get better. One writer I admire, Reinhold Schneider, called this your "commission."

HONOR

There is such a thing as Christian Honor.
—Georges Bernanos

As one biographer, Robert Speaight, introduces him as he arrived in London in 1944, passing through on the eve of his return to Paris, after six years of self-imposed exile in Brazil, speaking before an audience at the French Institute, where the audience had gathered as much to see him as to hear him—for these were long before the days, remember, when every famous person is a familiar face, an over familiar, in every home, and Georges Bernanos was a famous man. Here he was to look upon, "a man of burly physique and bronzed complexion, walking with the aid of a stick."

A Catholic writer whose ambition it was to be both totally in the world but not of it was George Bernanos, and Bernanos' ideal was honor. As Cardinal von Balthasar, in his book *Bernanos*, writes: "Bernanos could not give the ideal image of man always before him in his struggle a better and simpler name than that of *honor*. This concept was not for him one important value chosen from other possible ones; rather, honor was something like the absolute ethical foundation that imparts personal dignity, moral splendor, sublimity, and divine likeness to all the commandments and the fulfillment of the commandments. Honor was for Bernanos a shibboleth and a watchword." As Bernanos was the Catholic layman par excellence, so honor is the particular virtue of the laity and only the laymen can impart it: "'The disciplines of the Church,' he says, ' . . . are not enough to form the Christian knight . . . The Church is not a teacher of honor; she is a teacher of charity.'" And Bernanos rebukes repeatedly, with mounting exasperation, a clergy that has lost its honor: "In order to become a holy man, don't you think, you must first of all become a man?" Bernanos spoke of pride as well. "As Bernanos used it, it connotes not the arrogance of *orgueil*, but rather interior-mettle, noble-mindedness, and undaunted boldness of spirit." It is an aristocratic conception of life that he exalts and it is the only hope for the future. If the young wish "to become a second order of chivalry, it must begin by saving the notion and reality of honor."[125]

Catholic

In broad fashion, the tradition of Honor Psychology is the tradition of the Catholic Church. This is the Church the writings of whose Common Doctor, Thomas Aquinas, youngest son of a Norman military family, cousin to the Emperor, a finely-mannered Gentleman at heart, as Chesterton divined in the book that even Gilson called the finest written about St. Thomas, were called by Pope John Paul II, in a telling phrase, "The philosophy of the proclamation of being, a chant in praise of what exists." This is the Church whose true *apologia* Pope Benedict has said is our art and our Saints, to which I would in all humility add our Chivalry: *The Song of Roland*; Norman Knights, "the sword of the Papacy"; Baldwin IV, the Leper King of Jerusalem, the Lion Heart, El Cid, and, of course, that most chivalrous of Saints – he of "the Two Standards," St. Ignatius. ("The Spiritual Exercises and the Society of Jesus reveal themselves 'as it were, from below,' as the work of a nobleman and soldier. Their ideal is the 'more' of a chivalrous disposition, but one which developed into the discretion of service.")[126] This is the Church and the Tradition of the poets Gerard Manley Hopkins and "The Windhover": "oh air, pride, plume here Buckle!" and David Jones whose "Anathemata," with its astonishingly lovely portrait of Guinevere at Christmas Midnight Mass, Auden called the greatest long poem of the last century—" . . . all the numinous whole, over all the knit / parts other than the column of her neck and the span-broad / forehead and whatever strong enchantment lay between forehead / and chin . . . "— of Chesterton and Belloc, and Eric Gill, of Peguy, Claudel and Bernanos, of Reinhold Schneider, of de Lubac and von Balthasar, of Gilson and Maritain, of Sigrid Undset, Edith Stein and Dorothy Day, of McLuhan, Wilhemsen and Walter Ong. And it is the tradition of

Rudolf Allers, once Adler's foremost student and colleague and, for a time, the landlord of a young von Balthasar. What pleasure picturing them, entertaining each other, as they often did, in the evening, in the drawing room, taking turns at the piano, playing Bach and Mozart. And how symbolic, too!—psychology and theology "making beautiful music together." Let Allers stand for all those many Catholic psychologists—Viktor White, Adrian van Kaam, William Lynch, etc.—whose contributions have recently been chronicled by Robert Kugelmann in his Cambridge University-published *Psychology and Catholicism: Contested Boundaries.* Like Allers, they worked in the shadows of giants—Freud, Jung, and Adler—some, to some renown, but more in relative isolation, obscurity, or captious discontent. In sum this vision and these voices secure for Honor Psychology a noble, perhaps the noblest of them all, animating antecedent.

BELIEFS

The ethos of representation is noble; the ethos of self-fulfillment
by the person is bourgeois. The sense for rank and subordination
is noble; the idea of individuals' equality of value and rights is
bourgeois. The ethos of distance as respect for the other and as
an abiding form of love is noble; the ethos of closeness through a
"personal" relationship of familiarity and the ideal of the greatest possible directness is bourgeois. The ethos of service is noble
. . . Noble is the ideal that remains upwardly open . . .
                        —Hans Urs von Balthasar, *The Grain of Wheat*

I practice a long-term, action-based, meaning-finding therapy. It is
based on the premises that 1) all people more or less desire the same
things: that we want to be happy, decent people who lead productive,
fulfilling lives; and that we want the same for our children; that we
want to succeed at work and enjoy our families; that we want to live
in peace and be fair and compassionate to others; that we want to be
free to worship and to vote where and for whom we please; but that,
undeniably, 2) life is a battle—Theodore Roosevelt said that and so
did Henry David Thoreau, "*Militia est vita hominis super terram*,"
as the Good Book says, Job 7:1, the Latin Vulgate—that just as we
all desire more or less the same things, we nonetheless frequently
find ourselves beset and embattled, disappointed, fearful, stuck, hurt,
confused, suffering, afflicted, and in pain; so that 3) support in the
form of counseling can be useful—sometimes life saving, often, life
furthering—that is, the support of someone, trained and experienced
who listens and empathizes, who offers hope, encouragement, infor-

mation, direction, and guidance. A good counselor, in my view, models his core convictions and beliefs; cares for and about his clients; tries to encourage and inspire; and strategizes how best to cope, how best to run the race and fight the good fight, as St. Paul says, how best to endure and prevail, as William Faulkner said in his famous Nobel Prize acceptance speech, how best to win the battle of life. The goal of this model is enhanced self-respect, courage and self-control. The goal is honor.

My examples in this are many. I look back especially to St. Paul: " . . . Paul's relations with the Christian community are so rich that he can describe himself as their father, wet-nurse, teacher, friend and brother."[127]; to the Stoic "Doctors" whom he in some way recalls (see Stanley W. Jackson for a brief description of Stoic psychotherapy— for counsel, guidance and advice, seek out an older wiser man "who was commonly considered to be good and noble")[128]; to the great Spiritual Directors both of history and literature—St. Ignatius, who prized the gift of magnanimity; to the Cure de Torcy so memorably depicted in George Bernanos' great novel, *Diary of a Country Priest*, he of such a commanding but gentle presence: "Then we had another glass of gin together. And suddenly he looked me straight in the eyes, with complete assurance, commanding. He seemed to have become a different person, a man who would take orders from no one, an aristocrat."[129] Readers of the novel who knew Bernanos personally believed the Cure, whether intentionally or not, Bernanos' self-portrait. The Cure, to my mind, is the model honor therapist. In the tradition of psychology, I look to Alfred Adler, the goal of whose therapy has been described as "the imparting of thymos."[130]

Where all therapists actively listen, therapists inspired by these examples will try to actively speak, that is, to speak in such a way as to help clients tap into their inner strengths, notice their achievements, rally their spirits, revive their hopes, and recover their dignity. In this way therapists may seem to have something in common with preachers and poets, statesmen and generals whose purpose it is to improve morale, consolidate and strengthen purpose. People of my generation sometimes recall being unusually inspired by John F. Kennedy's inaugural speech or the words of Martin Luther King—some to the point of even changing their lives. An earlier generation remembered Winston Churchill and Roosevelt. Every great work of art, every great sermon and speech is always a call to action.

What does an Honor Psychologist believe? He believes that human beings have a spiritual orientation, that we are primordially ordained to the True, the Beautiful, the Good. He believes in the traditionalist worldview expressed in Faulkner, Eliot, and Yeats, as well as others—moderns such as Isak Dinesen or Georges Bernanos—and in the canon: the Bible, Homer, Dante, Shakespeare. An Honor Psychologist believes in Standards, especially that of the Lady and the Gentleman, grace and chivalry. "Beauty is more than appearance / more than radiance of face / It is also manners, gentleness, civility and grace."[131] He prizes magnanimity above all virtues. An Honor Psychologist believes in a realist, participatory, particularist though not relativistic, epistemology as is developed in Aristotelian-Thomistic and phenomenological-existential philosophy. Honor Psychology represents a psychology of the *agon*: Life is a battle: first, a struggle for survival—roof over your head, food on the table; then security—the comforts of atmosphere and home; for success—achievement and success and the hope that our children will surpass us; and, finally, significance—the significance of belonging, of belonging to another through the sacrament of marriage, the loyalty and mutual respect, to a family, to a place, to a community, culture, history, tradition. The basic drive in human beings is for permanence, the analogue in this life of eternity. The basic drive is for civilization. As Vico said in a fundamental distinction: "The barbarian can survive in nature but is incapable of making his home within it." Life is hard; it is never easy, so as St. John says, we must "harden ourselves in hope" and Winston Churchill: "Never flinch, never weary, never despair." Honor in all things. And yet, the honor psychologist knows as well that "though we speak with the tongues of men and angels and have not love, it is as nothing."

EXHORTATION

> Once Sullivan revealed that he planned to enter a Randall's Is-
> land track meet. MacArthur fired him up with a pep talk end-
> ing: "Don't come back unless you're a winner." Inspired, the
> bodyguard broke the track's hammer-throw record and, though
> he was the oldest man there, he was voted the meet's outstand-
> ing athlete. He recalls: "I think the General could talk *any*body
> into *any*thing."
>
> —William Manchester, *American Caesar*

To honor possesses two components. What distinguishes an honor
psychologist is the privilege of the preachers. As St. Gregory the Great
writes: " . . . in exhorting individuals great exertion is required to be
of service to each individual's particular needs . . . " Exhortation:
exhort: "To urge by earnest appeal or argument; advise or recommend strongly. To utter or give exhortation." It derives from having
a strong moral stance, from believing in something and speaking with
authority—even audacity—and believing other people should share
the liberation that comes with such certainty and conviction. Yes, "I
believe in One God . . . " And it derives from believing in what philosophy calls "the real distinction," that is, that existence can never
be reduced to essence, that we make ourselves through our choices,
that we are undeniably, irreducibly free. Exhortation, then, can only
be persuasive; it can never bind.

There is a time, a season, for honoring as Heideggerian *gelassenheit*,
for Ignatian *indifferencia*, for Rogerian reflection, for narrative collaboration, for Marian letting be, for therapist as honoring witness;
but there is also a time, a season, a perhaps more decisive time and
season, for Heideggerian resoluteness, for the Ignatian Two Stan-

dards, for Tillich's the courage to be, for Frankl's idealism, for Bernanos' militancy. "Stand erect, hold your heads high, because your Liberation is near at hand"(Luke 21:28). It is the moment of "do or die," of no excuses, no evasions, no dodges, get up, suck it up, prevail. Be the bigger person. Be the better person, keep faith with your promises, live up to your ideals. Be true to your word, to the Word, to the words of the great philosophers and poets, to those who gave their lives so that you might live; to Him who gave his Life so that you might have everlasting life. Do what you know and believe in your heart to be the right thing. Preserve your honor!

This comprises the second aspect of honoring. No one has ever expressed it more eloquently than de Saint-Exupery in the beautiful passage with which the French existential-phenomenologist Maurice Merleau-Ponty concludes *The Phenomenology of Perception*: "Your son is caught in the fire; you are the one who will save him . . . If there is an obstacle, you would be ready to give your shoulder provided only that you can charge down that obstacle. Your abode is your act itself. Your act is you . . . You give yourself in exchange . . . Your significance shows itself, effulgent. It is your duty, your hatred, your love, your steadfastness, your ingenuity . . . Man is but a network of relationships . . . "[132] Honor embraces the therapeutic need to at times exhort—to honor the eternal in man: "What is Man that thou art mindful of him / And the son of man that You visit him? / For You have made him a little lower than the angels, / And You have crowned him with glory and honor" (Psalms 8: 4-6)—by exhortation.

The Sickness unto Death

We all fear Hell don't we? Anxiety before the void, "the sickness unto death." Angst, dread, boredom, vertigo. Anxiety: it is at the heart, at the core, at the foundation of so much suffering. Delusions, psychosis, paranoia, schizophrenia, OCD, phobias of every sort, the life unlived because of waves of discomfort, the beating heart, the sweaty palms and underarms, the flushed or pallid face, the mania, the tension, stress, distress, the wallflower, the ne'er-do-well, dread, guilt, embarrassment, disgust, fear. Fearfulness, timidity, "Why can't he just do it?" "Why won't she go?"

An honor psychologist must confront this issue, must confront it face to face. I do it with von Balthasar, who once responded to Karl Barth's implicit accusation: "The Catholic doctrine is that there is a Hell, not that there is anybody in it." And, indeed, it was von Balthasar's first book that raised the question: "Can we dare to hope that all human beings are saved?" His answer was "Yes." So far as I follow his reasoning, it runs as follows (and seems to me, when addressed this way, irrefutable). As Catholics we believe in the Creed: "I believe in One God, the Father Almighty, Creator of Heaven and earth and in Jesus Christ, His Son, Our Lord . . . was crucified, died and was buried. He descended into hell . . . " Christ, our Lord, descended into hell . . . descended into Hell; therefore, in some mysterious way hell has been sacramentalized. Christ was in hell, so that those in hell can never be said to be lost to Christ, to be estranged and alienated from Him, alienated, finally, from His Love. As Christ, by becoming fully human, shared in all things human, sacramentalized them, so that he shared in our suffering and we are asked to share in his, to offer up our suffering, our pain, our anguish, our anxiety, so, again, in some mysterious way, Christ shares in the sufferings of the damned, except if He is present to them, and they to Him, are they truly damned?

Face your fear? Rise, above it? Yes! But even in that sickness unto death, even in that angst before the Void, that appears to be coextensive, consubstantial with human being-in-the-world, even amid that dread of Hell, be comforted, have faith. He descended into Hell. He is there with you. You cannot be lost. The Nothing, the Void, the Emptiness, the Valley of Death, the Inferno, the Gates of Hell, Hell itself: He is there. He will not abandon you. You cannot be lost. Bear with me. He bears and bears up us both.

GOALS

Man's real treasure is the treasure of his mistakes, piled up stone
by stone through thousands of years . . . Breaking the continuity
with the past, wanting to begin again, is a lowering of man . . .
It was a Frenchman, Dupont-White, who around 1860 had the
courage to exclaim: "Continuity is one of the rights of man: it is
a homage of everything that distinguishes him from the beast."
—José Ortega y Gasset, *Toward a Philosophy of History*

But what was symbol to the pagan, is reality for the Catholic.
The Mystical Body of Christ unites all ages into one company,
and I can talk to Augustine, not as to a memory, but as to a man.
—Frederick D. Wilhelmsen, *Citizen of Rome*

The goal of Life is to live in continuity with the best in one's own tradition in solidarity with the best in all others. What is the best of the
West? One of the best, and, certainly, one of the most dynamic, fertile,
characteristic, and enduring expressions—determining, possibly defining—is the idea of life as a struggle, of Life as a Battle. It emerges in
the Old Testament, in Job, *militia est vita homini* (a soldier's service
is the life of man); we encounter it in the Gospels—"I come to bring
a sword," in St. Paul—"fight the good fight," "run the race," strap on
the armor of God, and the Stoics—Seneca said "to live is to fight," in
Theodore Roosevelt and also Henry David Thoreau, in Henry James,
in Darwin, of course, and the sociobiology of Edward O. Wilson, and
in the Resolve (Heidegger) and Courage to Be (Tillich) of the existentialists. The Jesuit literary and cultural critic Walter Ong has written
a magnificent book about it, *The Contest for Life*—the idea that Life
is a Battle, that to live is to fight, augmented with the notion that the

struggle must be fought according to a standard: with chivalry. Here
we look to Belloc: "The City . . . and what we have come to call chivalry . . . these two are but aspects of one thing without a name; but
that thing all Europeans possess, nor is it possible for us to conceive
of a patriotism unless it be a patriotism which is chivalric. In our ear-
liest stories, we honor men fighting odds. Our epics are of small num-
bers against great; humility and charity are in them, lending a kind
of magic strength to the sword. The Faith did not bring in that spirit,
but rather completed it."[133] Other words that resonate with chivalry
are *arete* for the Greeks or happiness as John F. Kennedy defined
it, following on the Greeks. "Happiness," he said, "is the full use of
all one's powers along lines of excellence," or the Roman gravitas or
honor (Bernanos), pride as Isak Dinesen divined it—"Pride is the
loyalty that a man gives the idea that God had when he made him,"
virtue, as Huizinga presents it in *Homo Ludens*: excellence. I would
plant the flag with Aristotle and St. Thomas (and, incidentally, the
French psychologist, Robert Desoille) and posit as goal: magnanimity. Of St. Thomas, Gilson writes:

> It is a far cry from St. Thomas's man to the stunted human plant
> which some have imagined he would have him. He aimed at the
> cultivation of the whole man, including his passions. He assigns
> him virtues whose object is to provide strength for the conquest
> of happiness. St. Thomas loves the daring, provided their dar-
> ing be good, for it must be so to undertake great things and to
> succeed in them. There must also be that confidence (*fiducia*)
> which authorizes the magnanimous man to rely upon his own
> strength and on the help of his friends. Confidence in self is a
> form of hope. It is a kind of fortitude. It is the strength which the
> magnanimous man draws from the just evaluation of the means
> at his disposal and from the hopes they inspire in him. And just

as he does not despise his own worth, neither does the magnanimous man despise the goods of fortune. The matter of the soul's
greatness is honor; its end is the doing of something great. Now
wealth attracts the crowd, itself sometimes a useful force, and
wealth is a powerful means of action, at least in a certain order
and for the attaining of certain ends. This eulogy of self-confi-
dence, of wealth, of love of honor and glory, does not come from
the fifteenth-century court of some prince of the Italian Renaissance but from a thirteenth-century monk with vows of poverty
and obedience..[134]

Existentialists call this "authenticity." Contemporary positive psychologists might call it "flourishing."

LETTER TO A YOUNG PSYCHOLOGIST

Holed up in a windowless hotel conference room near Washington D.C., scientists have been busy rewriting the bible of American Mental Illness . . . Each expert must agree to limit their involvement with drug companies to $10,000 over the duration of the revision. About a third of the experts invited to join committees declined to do so for this reason . . .

—"Mental Illness Gets a Rethink for Kids," *Wall Street Journal*, October 19, 2012

A book recommendation for you: *Psychology's Ghosts*, by Jerome Kagan, Harvard Emeritus. If one could speak of "the greatest living American psychologist," it might very well be Jerome Kagan. Excellent vintage, flavor, wonderful full-bodied fruit of a long, distinguished career—not a debunking exactly, but well-reasoned dissent from "research" oriented, neuro-psychology, brain, etc. orientation. Kagan develops these points and they are essential for you to remember: 1) psychological realities are more or less immeasurable; 2) all human experience is meaningful; 3) meaning is always cultural, class and experience bound. Scientific "research" does not allow for this—there exists the problem of replication, decline effect, etc. Typical treatment does not allow for this either, especially the prescription of psychiatric medication, which is premised on "one size fits all." Kagan debunks the DSM—it is just a list and groupings of overlapping symptoms but symptoms cannot be understood outside of human context—again, culture, class, history, Faith, language, experience, meaning, age and maturity level, etc. I would add that the truth of symptoms is unlikely to ever be candidly and comprehensively disclosed except in the context of a trusting, honoring relationship. Regardless of the sophistication of their methods and tools, researchers will never fathom these depths.

Truly, what is psychology?—the speech and meaning not of the soul—this, in my rather presumptuous view, was Jung and Hillman's great mistake. No. Psychology is the speech and meaning—psyche logos—of this soul, your soul, my soul, in this body, this history, this culture, this class, at this age, speaking this language, in this Church, with this faith. And what is psychological work? It is the effort to extend one's understanding, self-understanding, of all the elements that shape, form, condition, determine, sustain, uphold and potentially uplift us and to develop a relationship to them. You must wrestle with your history—your history is your Angel, your limit and gift—with both its blessing and its curse. What comprises the goal of psychological work? We call it flourishing now (I like that word! It is one of Yeats' favorites: he prays that his daughter may "flourish like a linnet tree"). It is to live in continuity with the best in one's culture and history in solidarity with the best in all cultures and histories i.e. the Natural Law, "the old verities," (Faulkner), "the permanent things" (Eliot). In any case, my friend, it is to this understanding of psychology that I have devoted my career and life.

We have the Boulder Model, the Vail Model. I would propose the Vatic Model. Yes, the psychologist should be a Scholar as the Vail model asserts (forgive me, I cannot take the Boulder model seriously— a Scientist-Practitioner, really? What kind of world has science given us? O Brave New World, indeed. I like the comforts and conveniences, going to the doctor and the dentist, the miracle drugs but I do fear, upon my very soul I fear it, we have laid waste the world, are poisoning the planet, kill babies in the womb, torture animals— you know Pope Benedict coined a wonderful phrase about animals:

he called them "our companions in creation"—and call it medical research. I think Bernanos was right about technology. You ought to read him. As you can see in my politics I am a kind of pro-life Green, a Red Tory); a consumer of research, a skilled Practitioner: but what kind of scholar? What kind of research? What kind of practitioner? I would make him a Knight-Scholar—we Catholics are forever dreaming of chivalry, Peguy, Claudel, Bernanos, Reinhold Schneider, not to speak of Chesterton and Belloc and Fritz Wilhelmsen; a Don Quixote, who reads as quest, for edification, for inspiration, for transformation really, for utility, precedent, example, model, a quixotic Quixote forever in search for Dulcinea—the soul of the text. Tillich made the Knight emblematic of his existentialism; Hillman, the knight errant, of his erudite soul psychology—I always liked Hillman's "we don't need a language fashioned in schools; we need a language that is schooled and fashioned." Norman O. Brown fifty years ago in a famous Phi Beta Kappa speech delivered at Columbia invoked Emerson—and I think Emerson speaks somewhere about scholarship as chivalry—on this. If you intend to be a scholar, be an American Scholar in Emerson's sense. A consumer of research, yes, that too: but research into the geography, travails, the sufferings and splendor of the human spirit, of the human condition in all its misery and glory. Read all the research, yes, quantitative, qualitative, narrative, but read the poets Yeats, Eliot, Jeffers and whomever speaks to you, and the novelists—Bernanos, of course, and Conrad, Melville, Faulkner, and the Homer of our era, Cormac McCarthy; read history—Burckhardt, Huizinga, Lukacs; biography—Manchester on Churchill, MacArthur, and Kennedy; Thomas Merton's *Seven Story Mountain*, Augustine's *Confessions*. Read like Bobby Kennedy did, upon the murder of his brother, out of a desperate desire to understand:

RFK was a sensualist who craved brilliant sunlight and the sea.
But he appears to have spent much of the vacation holed up in
his room reading a book given to him by Jackie, Edith Hamilton's
The Greek Way . . . But it was RFK who found the most lasting relief from (the book) . . . It is easy to imagine Kennedy, desperate
for some meaning in senseless tragedy, transfixed by the moral
extracted from the historians Herodotus and Thucydides and the
playwrights Aeschylus, Sophocles, and Euripides . . . Reading
these words in the cool dark of his room, as the brilliant light of
the Caribbean illuminated the sea beyond—as the radiance of
the Aegean had shone for the Greeks in an earlier millennium—
Kennedy must have wondered if the great historians were speaking directly to him.[135]

And skilled practitioner? Yes,—skilled, yes: I can break it down
as: model, care about and for your clients, support empathize and
comfort, inspire, encourage, and, yes, sometimes, exhort, strategize.
I can sum it up as an exercise in phronesis, practical wisdom, the
application of common sense (read Gadamer here on the *sensus communis*). It is prudence that you need. You will need to practice the
virtue of prudence.

The great problem is not so much to know what prudence is, but
to acquire it. It is a life's work. It is a far cry from the practical
experience garnered by individual men in the give and take of
daily life which we commonly call prudence to the carefully and
patiently constructed virtue of prudence of St. Thomas. In order
to become prudent it is necessary to set about it early and delib-
erately. Experience is necessary, and so is memory. The memory
must be trained by being made to accumulate useful data and
then frequently to recall it so as not to lose it. There are habits of
intellect, too, which are indispensable to the prudent and which

must be carefully cultivated. In sum, in deciding every particular case he must know how to begin, in order to arrive at its ends. What he has to acquire in order to become prudent is the ability to discern the particular act that must be done if the desired result in a given case is to be obtained . . .

This is truly an art . . . There must be acquired as well a sort of special sense which is the privilege of a reason long accustomed to move among the details of the concrete case and effectively to resolve practical problems. Everything has to be put to work in order to acquire this quality . . . It is a practical presence of mind . . . Reasoning, foresight, circumspection, precaution are all essential elements of prudence, and there is no real prudence without them.[136]

As Gilson explains, prudence is a special sense, a sixth sense, a third ear. It takes time to develop. It is a feel for things. Von Balthasar thought the modern idea of feeling was a recapitulation of the ancient doctrine of the "spiritual senses." It is a sixth sense. It is being human—all-too-human, yes (do you know that story about Nietzsche first meeting the diva Lou Andreas-Salome in a Cathedral, "Lady, what star have you fallen from?"). "Play with more humanity"—that was Sibelius' instructions to the Orchestra on the occasion of conducting his final symphony. Be prudent, be human, be all-too-human, "play with more humanity." Prudence is the right feeling; it is the right touch. Let people think you a little "touched"—they'll find (your clients, that is), you'll find, together with your vulnerability, that it makes you human, available, approachable. Two questions to ask yourself if you wish to become a therapist. First, do people often stop and ask you for directions? And do you like to talk, to talk all day, and, sometimes, into the wee hours of the morning? If the answer is yes, you probably have what it takes. And, then, speak, but always from your heart, authentically, sincerely, with the frank boldness of the born aristocrat, but with the meekness of the Saint, and the humility of the beggar, speaking from and by and to the heart, the soul, the spirit. Speak with the authority that your quest, like RFK's, your reading, the breadth and depth of your knowledge will confer upon you and instill and inspire you with. Go to Mass, pray the Rosary, Confess. Stay close to the Sacraments. When you stray they will bring you back. E. E. Cummings said: "I have to fight every day to be myself." You'll have to fight every day to be this kind of psychologist. But as Krishna said to Arjuna after showing him the panorama of human life as a battlefield: "Fight on!" It's a good job. I like it. As Sean Connery says in the movie *Cuba,* about being a soldier of fortune: "It is an honorable profession."

To be Psychological

To be "psychological" means to be intensely intellectual, thoroughly philosophical, impressionistic, intuitive, improvisational, imaginative, ambitiously—like Bernanos, like Faulkner, like Lorca, like Yeats—imaginative. It means to be experiential, phenomenological, empathetic, attentive as a poet, or, St. Thomas, to particulars and the sensory dimension—"O Taste and See"—and the beauty and honor and strength, the essential nobility, that have remained invisible, glimpsed, if glimpsed at all, through a glass darkly, as St. Paul says. It means being attentive to the vice hidden in every virtue and the virtue hidden in every vice. It means the realization that "the good news and the bad news is the same news." It means being steeped in the march and magnificence of history and tradition, in thrall to the glory of the arts, in awe and fascinated by those sweeping, ubiquitous patterns that echo hauntingly and reverberate through history, like signs and miracles, like the beating of an angel's wings or the footsteps of the gods. It means to be reverent before ancient ritual and rite and the world's Great Religions; irreverent in the face of cant, intolerance, hypocrisy. It means remembering that what is most important in life is usually immeasurable no matter how sophisticated the methodology or instrument. It means to be rhetorical in speech and prose and poetic in vision, for this is the language and vision of the soul. Psychology, to be psychological, to be the logos of the soul, must express the soul. And, finally, to be psychological means to reach out to God, in the way of the Psalmist, with fear and trembling, passion and joy, wondering all the while "What is Man that Thou art mindful of him?" for the soul is primordially ordained to God, to the three great Transcendentals: Truth, Goodness, and Beauty. As St. Augustine says, "My soul is restless until it rests in Thee," as he also says "O Beauty, too late have I loved Thee." This is psychology: nothing less suffices.

Psychological Learning

> For the ancients, to meditate is to read a text and to learn it
> "by heart" in the fullest sense of this expression, that is, with
> one's whole being: with the body, since the mouth pronounced
> it, with the memory which fixes it, with the intelligence which
> understands its meaning and with the will which desires to put
> it into practice.
>
> —Jean Leclercq, *The Love of Learning and The Desire for God*

To read psychology the way some people once read natural science, theology, history, or law; that is, with a devotion to truth, a thirst for the Eternal, a fascination with precedent, example, and application; to learn as the old French saying about how to learn to jump a horse: "Throw your heart across the fence first, the horse will follow"; to practice within the framework of the classical analogy between state and soul so just as it is the responsibility of the statesman, the *strategos*, to care for welfare of the state, so it is the duty of the psychologist is to care for welfare of the soul; to listen hour after hour to the human soul profess its dreams, pour out its woes and sorrows, is an honorable profession.

To read so broadly, widely, copiously, comprehensively is to inevitably realize that there is nothing new under the sun, that we all repeat something—history, myth, pattern, plot, type, cycle; that we all lead representative lives; but still the existential moment remains, the moment of life and death, the moment that we choose, life or death, the culture of life or the culture of death. I choose the culture of life in John Paul II's sense, and in psychology I choose depth over surface; directive over non-directive, meaning over the absurd; the system (family) over individuals; and in the ancient rivalry of art and science, I choose art, culture, the Humanities, Imagination. For myself I choose a Christian Humanism; I choose Adler and his psychology of *thymos*; I choose "reasonablesness and chivalry" (Belloc), a worldly wisdom that is a force for good. I choose virtue. I choose honor.

Master Spirits

> Nothing gives me so much pleasure as my ability to extricate
> from the chaos of history the four or five figures who together
> represent for me the constellation of my own ideas and mission.
>
> —Hans Urs von Balthasar, *The Grain of Wheat*

A long-term, confidence-building, action-oriented, meaning-finding therapy—a therapy of honor and encouragement and strategy and sympathetic understanding, of magnanimity, one might say—from what I would call an Honor Psychology orientation, with children and teens, individuals, families and couples: that's what I do. As precursor and precedent—to whom I always look, believing, as I do, that there is, in general, nothing new under the sun, I honor and depend—stand on the shoulders, if you will, of all the great predecessors: Freud and Jung and Adler, especially. Adler's inspiring effect on patients is reported again and again by people who encountered him—Manes Sperber, the famous novelist, said that Adler gave him back his courage. Also Viktor Frankl for his emphasis on ideals and personal responsibility—Frankl use to say that the Statue of Liberty on our East Coast ought to be balanced by a Statue of Responsibility on the West Coast; Frankl, too, in a pun I much admire referred to practitioners of his school as "stretches" as opposed to "shrinks": their duty being to encourage patients to "self-distance" and "self-transcend," that is, to reach beyond themselves for meaning; most recently I have studied the formidable and cerebral Murray Bowen, one of the founders of Family Therapy, immersing myself in the Bowenian perspective—the novelist Isak Dinesen used to quote a French saying that "If you want to learn to jump a horse, throw your heart over the fence first, the horse will follow,"—which is the optimal way to study, with deep appreciation and benefit; also Ivan Bozormenyi Nagy with his emphasis on justice, his integrative approach and his idea of mental health as "constructive entitlement," as close an approximation as I can find in our tradition to what I mean by honor; Milton Erickson, whom Jay Haley called "the Picasso" of therapy—and James Hillman, who was once my teacher, who, in many ways, stands alone in the history of psychology, in sheer breadth and brilliance of scholarship and style. Wordsworth wrote a poem in which he honored his great predecessor English poets as "master spirits." The aforementioned have been mine.

NEO-ADLERIAN

Deep reflection is a conversation of one's self with one's thymos
or one's thymos with one's self.
    —Richard Onians, *The Origins of European Thought*

In some respects honor psychology may be understood as a neo-Adlerian psychology. More than any other psychologist Adler understood that to gain your life you must lose it. Adler posited significance (honor), to depend upon belonging to something larger than one's self, which he called *gemeinschaftsgefuhl*, a word best translated as a "feeling for the whole." "Particularly it means feeling with the whole, *sub specie aeternitatis*, under the aspect of eternity." Mental health, self-acceptance, self-esteem (significance) depend upon self-transcendence. Adler exalted courage as the soul of mental health, so much so that one of his keenest interpreters, Alexander Neuer, described Adler's psychology as a psychology of *thymos*—a Greek word in some ways equivalent to what Bernanos called honor—and the object of Adlerian therapy to be the transmission of *thymos*. According to Neuer:

> Adler calls courage (Mut) that kind of higher psychic energy, or *thymos*, which the ancient Greeks considered the essence of the soul. To impart *thymos* . . . will be the basic concern of the educator, as well as the psychotherapist, regardless, whether his patient is a child or an adult.[137]

In therapy Adler was confident and directive: "The patient must be guided away from himself, toward productivity for others; he must be educated toward social interest; he must be led from his seclusion from the world, back to existence; he must be brought to the only correct insight, that he is as important for the community as anyone else; he must get to feel at home on this earth." Therapist is educator, guide, leader, persuader, director. But at the same time understated, friendly, tactful, cheerful, jovial: "You must be as unprepossessed as possible toward the patient." Psychotherapy " . . . requires trained sagacity and ingenuity, a jovial attitude . . . blessed with cheerfulness and good humor . . . also extreme patience and forbearance." " . . . consolation, encouragement and redeeming power." He called his therapeutic technique: encouragement. "Adler never encouraged without laying open the problem for the solution of which courage was to be used. Not encouragement in itself, but balance of encouragement and responsibility was Adler's formula."[138] An admirer and student of the canon—the Bible, Shakespeare, Dostoevski, Adler appropriated the tradition of the commonplace ("In the course of times one gathers a collection of slogans.") and mined the tradition for its pearls of wisdom: "It is necessary to have a series of dramatic illustrations at one's disposal. These are more effective than sober expositions. I am thinking here of Shaw's *Androcles and the Lion*." Finally, for Adler the change that therapy promotes can be described as the supersession of a constricted, self-bounded imagination by a more gracious, magnanimous one intent on service, contribution, engagement, participation. "The cure or reorientation is brought about by the destruction of the faulty picture of the world and unequivocal acceptance of a mature picture of the world." And "The cure can come about only when there is a reconciliation with the problems of life: that is, through the recognition of the faulty life style and strengthening of social interest, an important share of which are contribution and courage to face life." Significance, self-transcendence, belonging to something greater than one's self, courage, *thymos*, directive, but understated, encouraging, magnanimity: honor psychology is a neo-Adlerian psychology.

COUNTER–CULTURE CATHOLIC THERAPIST

The society of which St. Thomas is thinking is different in structure from free-trade societies where everything is a matter of trade and commerce and of a trade regulated by the law of supply and demand . . . St. Thomas would never admit that trade could legitimately control, as happens in a capitalistic society, the exchange and distribution of goods necessary for life . . . What governs the question is the fact that every man has the right by natural law to the means necessary for existence. To make a profit on a right is an injustice.

—Etienne Gilson, *The Christian Philosophy of St. Thomas*

My life was very conventional . . . Having a conventional marriage enabled me to be free intellectually.

—Norman O. Brown in *Walking with Nobby:*
Conversations with Norman O. Brown

Before it degenerated into sex, drugs, rock and roll, or was corrupted by the boomers whose avarice was on bold display from the first appearance of hippies *cum* yuppies, the message of the 60s counter-culture had a lot to recommend it. Like Jesus, the counter-culture was just all right with me. And despite all the excess and narcissism and the fact that the 60s are now a long time gone, a half century past, that message survives: it survives and continues to exercise considerable influence through the agency of the contemporary helping professions, through the ubiquity of what has been called "the therapeutic mind."

What is that message as it is shared today and was articulated in Theodore Rozak's landmark book, *The Making of the Counter-Culture*, where it receives its most in-depth and decisive formulation? The migration of the counter-culture into the helping professions limns something of an up-to-date answer of which I am reminded every time I satisfy my continuing education requirements for licensure by attending a workshop presented by a colleague.

The elements are these:

1) Get some spirituality in your life. Break out of the bounds of your ego. Open your heart to the rhythms of the cosmos. Self-transcend. Self-distance. Find meaning. Be mindful of the small things. Appreciate beauty. Stop and smell the roses. Manage your stress through relaxation, visualization, self-hypnosis, breathing, prayer.

2) Unload the guilt. Guilt is corrupting, destructive. Human beings make mistakes. Guilt does nothing good. Don't brood, obsess; let it go, put it behind you.

3) Grieve your losses. Much of depression is masked grief. Grieve, cry, surrender, say good-bye, let go. Pass through the stages: shock, anger, depression, bargaining, resolution.

4) Practice kindness. Find meaning, let go of your guilt and grieve and then do as much good as you can. The small things count. Do something nice today for someone else. Surprise them. Give gifts, remember birthdays, holidays. Tell people that you love them.

5) Be socially conscious. Get involved. Join a group. Help a charity. Do a charity walkathon. Be politically aware. Be a voice and a vote.

6) Set good boundaries and maintain them. Don't let people push you around. Stand up for yourself, speak out. Communicate. Don't enable or be co-dependent.

7) Reject and resist as best you can the soul-deadening, soul-destroying conformities required by modern life. Don't be a cog in the

wheel, be a citizen in your community, be a good neighbor. Think globally, act locally.

8) Teach the children well. Parent for peace. Honor childhood and all the virtues of childhood—wonder, joy, innocence, creativity, etc. And honor the elders.

What it all add ups to is this: live holistically, in touch with the spirit, free of guilt, able to say good-bye and move on, practicing kindness, socially conscious, autonomous and individual, human in the best sense.

Whether promoted by the best of the 60s counter-culture or encountered today in the helping professions, this philosophy and ethic merit respect.

The question is, how do you do it? The 60's failed as a genuine social and spiritual transformation because it didn't have a persuasive and practical answer. The communes closed. Woodstock became Altamont. Dionysus returned, alright, as Brown and Marcuse wanted him to, but in the guise of Charles Manson, that is, with a knife that was soaked in blood. Just about every workshop I have attended in the last thirty years (there is some selectivity in this: I avoid trainings that sound boring and they sound the more boring to me to the degree that they are DSM-oriented, but, in reality, not that many are, presumably because what sounds boring to me sounds boring to most other clinicians) addresses, in one roundabout way or another, one of the main counter cultural ideals. The objective is always to elaborate ways that participants in the workshop can help their clients meet the aforementioned needs—to find meaning and spirituality, let go of guilt and grief, etc.—and how the participants might better meet these needs in their own lives. The cogency and coherence of the underlying philosophy is rarely expounded because it is more or less assumed that everyone participating shares it. On the whole, my experience has been that this is a reasonable assumption. The advice, techniques and information offered are generally sound, helpful, useful, ready to apply and stimulating to think about.

What I inevitably end up thinking on the trip home is how lucky I am to be in the field, to have the opportunities I do, the ability to make a living counter-culturally, in some continuity and solidarity with the ideals of my youth—I turned 14 in the Summer of Love— the ability to live with integrity, that is some real unity between the life I have built for myself and my family and the practice of my profession.

I also thank God that I'm Catholic, that such grace has been given to me, because, as a believing, practicing Catholic the means to achieve these counter-culture ideals are given to me through the practice of my faith. I don't mean this to be too much of a Catholic apologia, so let me merely impressionistically indicate that if the goal is keeping faith with each of these ideals one can:

1) Get some spirituality in your life by going to Mass every day, surrendering oneself to the beauty, the wonder of it, the cadences and courtesies, the ancient prayers; say the Rosary, practice any of the spiritual disciplines and practices recommended by the Church. The true apologia for the Catholic Church, said Pope Benedict, is our art and our Saints.

2) Let go of guilt by going to Confession, the Sacrament of Reconciliation.

3) Catholics are very good with grief: the Rosary, the Funeral Mass, saying prayers, lighting candles, having Masses said for the departed; All Soul's Day when, at least in my Parish, Mass is still celebrated at the cemetery, an acknowledgment of the Community of Souls, our dead are always with us.

4) Kindness—the Golden Rule, the Beatitudes, the famous passage from St. Paul, that "the greatest of these is love."

5) To be socially conscious, committed to social and economic justice, read the great Papal Encyclicals, support the Catholic Worker movement that began with Dorothy Day, become a Distributist in the way of Chesterton and Belloc. These writings and movements are vintage counter-cultural, as Allen Watts, perhaps the greatest of the 60s gurus, acknowledged in his warmly appreciative eulogy to Chesterton.

6) For the need to maintain good boundaries, militantly, that is assertively at times, we Catholics have the ancient code of chivalry. One can read the great novelist Bernanos on honor or follow the example of Dorothy Day. Panther or Weatherman, Muslim or Malcolm X would understand Bernanos and Belloc.

7) To be a Catholic is to refuse to be a cog in the wheel; it is to insist always on the primacy of the person, a person with an immeasurable depth, a transcendent spirit, an irreplaceable worth.

And . . .

8) We do teach our children well. Father Andrew Greeley once said that the greatest contribution that Catholic Faith and Culture has made to America is the Parish School. Catholic schools have an unimpeachable record of saving and salvaging kids and the wreckage of lives on the shoals of poverty and disadvantage like none other. And we have pioneered home schooling. And for the old: perhaps the practice of the Faith is the greatest consolation. In our Church Hierarchy—well, as far as advancement is concerned, our priests in their fifties remain young men. For good or for ill, the leadership of the Church is a gerontocracy. Pope John Paul II insisted on dying publicly in rebuke to the modern Western tendency to sequester and abandon the Old. We do honor our Elders.

That Catholic Faith and Culture is a counter-culture, a counter-culture with multiple correspondences with the best of the 60s and with the best of the 60s as it has survived in the helping professions is, it seems to me, true, or, at least, a defensible proposition worthy of consideration.

The sad fact, however, is that while I feel generally at home when I attend a training workshop because of the correspondences I'm describing, I nearly always remain silent. The image of the Catholic Church—indeed, of nearly all institutional religion—that exists in all too many minds, especially of mental health professionals, is not an inclusive nor an inviting one. The Church is often viewed as a rigid, backward, oppressive, anti-female, stultifying, benighted institution, a concentration of the forces of reaction, which undeniably it is—a fierce force of reaction not only to the excess and narcissism of the modern world, but to the very agents against which the 60s counter-culture rose up in protest: the bureaucracies and banalities, the noise, the speed, the facelessness, the uniformities and standardizations, the dehumanization, the spiritual emptiness and privations of our modern world. And among Catholics the argument that the Church is counter-cultural, or, ought to be if faithful to its Tradition and Mission, is met with consternation if not sharp disagreement bordering on outrage.

The misunderstanding, it seems to me, boils down to sex and reproductive rights. But here there is irony. The most strident advocates of "pro choice" and what was once called "sexual liberation" are often in their private lives and in their families anything but permissive. The great Theodore Roszak a few years ago wrote with great tenderness about, among the boomers, the rediscovery of loyalty as integral to love. And the Catholic Tradition as expressed in the works of our greatest theologians, Saints, and lay writers, as well as in the Confessional, is exceptionally understanding and forgiving of the exigencies of sexual passion and the cruel, insoluble dilemmas confronting the modern family. The Priest whose instruction prepared me for my conversion—this in 1972—once told me that he thought contraception and abortion were more than anything cries of hopelessness. And, hope, the great Catholic poet Charles Peguy insisted, is the most rare and difficult of virtues.

Once in a great long while, in response to some event upon the public stage, the counter-culture unites. Though it is now yesterday's news, I was struck by the fact that during the 2012 Republican Presidential primary the tragic, tender story of the Santorums in their grieving of their lost child whose body they brought home from the hospital so that the child could be grieved by the baby's siblings and their decisions to birth and lovingly parent a child almost certain, barring a miracle, to not live long, incurred, at the time, a similar response from mental health professionals and from Catholics. A few days after this story first was publicized I was at a two-day training. And the story was repeatedly discussed. We understand. We acknowledge it as right and just and moving and deeply, indescribably admirable, and, profoundly, and terribly, human—human in the sense of as made in the Divine Image as much as any human act can be. Such concord of feeling, such unity in response between the Catholic and the therapeutic mind is admittedly unusual, but not unheard of. It might occur more. It should.

But it probably won't—not with the current division of society, a division aggravated and inflamed by the politicization of almost everything, a development resisted by the counter-culture in both its original 60s and Catholic form, a counter-culture that exalts the spiritual, the personal, the socially and economically just. But stranger things have happened. Or it may not. Common cause does not mean fraternity and friendship, or even mutual understanding and support, but a common cause it is, between the counter-culture of the contemporary helping professions and the counter-culture of the Catholic Church, both inching their way ineluctably, to, in the magnificent phrase of Theodore Rozak, the title of his sequel to *The Making of the Counter Culture*, "Where the Wasteland Ends." I'm glad to belong to this counter-culture, to have the luck and the grace to be a part of it both by profession and profession of faith. I'm glad to be what I have called an honor therapist, a counter-culture Catholic therapist.

HONORING THE VOW

The heart of marriage is the vow—the "for better and for worse," the "in sickness and in health"—the vow that we pledge to honor. Spouses honor their vows by remembering that a vow, a sacred vow before God and Church, is a pledge to act in time, to be totally in the world, but not of it—and in the world means totally, all in, the way a poker player is all in, pushing all his holdings to the center, rendering them subject, at the mercy of, the turn of the card. To be totally in the world but not of it means to be totally subject, in thrall to the beauties of creation, the drama and the pain, the roses and the thorns and to strive to sacramentalize (fill with the Spirit, bring closer to God, honor, and thus co-redeem) them. To be totally in the marriage means to be totally subject to it, to its risks, changes, and uncertainties, which is what the vow intends. Nothing in a marriage is set in stone; there is no status quo. The pledge, the honor, of the marriage resides in the commitment to grow—to grow together or to grow apart. As von Balthasar reminds us: "Everything remains suspended; nothing human ought to become entrenched and hardened. Just think of the relationship between lovers . . . "

Marriage is a temple with four pillars: the first is intimacy or shared vulnerability; second, satisfaction, that is, the mutual meeting of needs; third is fairness, which means a sense of fairness in the distribution of rights and responsibilities in the sharing of a life together; fourth is communion, which includes the joys of sex, of course, but more inclusively, and more fundamentally, enjoyment of and comfort in one another's physical presence. Couples who abide happily in this temple often describe their relationship as "We're close (intimacy); we match up pretty well (satisfaction); we get along (fairness); we like each other's company (communion)." Of course, the ground for these goods, the solvent, the "that without which" the others are impossible is effective communication, which means speaking with candor, conviction, clarity, and sensitivity to the other's needs and concerns, what a therapist might call, as Christ did, "the ability to hear" something. And, then, what is perhaps the ultimate form of communication: silence—a meaningful, valuable, comfortable silence. As Dietrich Bonhoeffer wrote, from a prison cell, in a Christmas letter to his fiancé: "Absolve me from talking about myself; I know I can't give you anything that will lend substance to your life other than a request to abide with me, go with me, and be my beloved wife and 'helpmate' just as I shall be your loving husband."[139] The goal is to sacramentalize a life together: to make one's own marriage a visible symbol of enduring, forgiving, though often fretful, disappointed, weary, tested, love.

Family Honor

To strive for one's own perfection is a bourgeois ideal. The bourgeois social climber must concentrate on getting ahead in the
world . . . The noble person knows nothing of all this because his
honor does not primarily depend on his person but his family . . .
Now, what God wants from every soul is a noble not a bourgeois
mentality. He desires service and a sense of service.

—Hans Urs von Balthasar, *The Grain of Wheat*

Catholic teaching maintains that the family, not the individual, is
the basic unit of society. This represents Aristotelian and Thomistic
thinking as well. If the old analogy between the order of society and
the order of the soul proves true, then we must reason that the family is also fundamental to the soul, a matter of "ultimate concern" in
Tillich's sense, a core, constitutive reality.

To honor the individual, then, to honor a soul, is also to honor
the family. An honor psychologist, a Catholic soul counselor, can't
help—if he is to honor his vocation—but also be a family therapist. I
think one honors family best by thinking of the family not so much
as a group of people conferred with in a consulting room, but as a
way of seeing, a perspective, a focus, a point of view. Honor therapy
as family therapy fulfills a way of seeing that identifies and privileges particular themes such as loss and love, loyalty, and continuity
(Bowen), communication and feeling (Satir), justice and entitlement
(Bozormenyi Nagy), creativity, madness, and the absurd (Whitaker),
power, structure, and hierarchy (Erickson, Minuchin, Haley) and
narrative (Michael White).

How does an honor therapist honor families? By reminding them that just as we all, as Shakespeare said, owe God a death, so we too owe a debt to our family; that we ought to think of ourselves as representative of our family, of our family's good name, of their reputation, of their honor; that a thought that warrants introduction into every decision-making process consists of: "How will this reflect on my family?"; that a very good reason not to do something contemplated is: "It would embarrass my family." This is a Roman way of seeing. The existential Thomist Frederick D. Wilhelmsen writes with inspired eloquence:

> To the old Roman at his best (and at his worst) the family is knit together by blood and a common land turned over by hands that have received their patrimony from a line of ancestors stretching back to the youth of the race. The dusk falls on the back of each man as he retreats down the road of time, but as he has received from the past, so has he given to the future, and as they lived in him, so shall he live in them. And this is promised him by the household gods, and even when he no longer believes in gods he still keeps them, for they are the badge of his service and the pledge of his immortality.[140]

And, as I said, it is a Catholic, Aristotelian, Thomistic, psychological way of thinking. The impact on therapy is to render sincere, authentic, authoritative what I have come to call "the Family Question":

"How do you think this might reflect on your family—and not even really just those living, and, certainly, not just those living in the house with you right now, or the son or daughter whom you are so adamant must see you, follow your rules, or the senior—I prefer to call them elders—whom you really ought to visit more, probably even take into your home: I mean, if you will consider it for a moment as a little more than half-crazy, I mean the Dead and those to come. In the Church, we call it 'the Community of Souls,' which means the Dead really are with us and that they are closer to God than we are. I mean have you ever thought about all those generations who have sweated, and cried, and suffered and worked, and sacrificed, so that you could be here today? Maybe your Mom or Dad didn't/hasn't done such a great job, but somebody, maybe long, long past, has done a great job or you wouldn't be here. And what about those who are still to come? How do you want them to look back at you, remember you?—with pride, a chuckle, a whispered prayer of gratitude that you were there when they needed you, that you thought way ahead through the generations, with foresight and tenderness? Do you want them to shake their heads with wonder at all you did? At what you stood for? At what you sacrificed? At what you achieved? Do you want them to honor you? Your memory? As someone who thought of their family? As someone who thought of their family first? Who thought at all of their family? That's what maintaining the family honor is all about. The Greeks wrote about it, Faulkner, Georges Bernanos. They all saw clearly that the family exists through time, a procession, a long march, and that clinging together, loving together, respecting each other, building for the future, being blessed by the past and blessing the future in turn is the best way to live, to flourish—flourish—that's kind of the shrink term now, flourish: to fulfill your destiny, to meet the challenge, win the battle, endure and prevail. It's up to you. And I know this sounds like a pep talk. A Greek philosopher might say it's addressed to your thymos, that part of you that stands fast, stands tall, stands up for what you believe in, and speaks up about what is right and just. Think about it. I'm not asking you to give up yourself, your own dreams, your own needs for that matter—they count too—but give some thought to your family's honor. Maybe come up with a motto—that's a very, very aristocratic thing to do, but the Scottish Clans did it too, and they were hardly aristocrats. Your family counts. And they ought to count with you."

Family honor.

HONORING

It is an artistic task.
—Alfred Adler on psychotherapy

In they come, tense, fretful, agitated, faces creased, fingers flexing, bottoms shifting in the chair. Each is locked in their own space, as if it were a cage, unable to comfort each other or reach out. A man and a woman, fortyish, well-groomed. With them, walking behind, is an eight year-old boy, shirt-tail out, probably re-pulled out on the three steps from the waiting room to my office. He is watchful, slightly dazed, sits down, fidgets.

I begin by reassuring them that we'll talk today as long as we need, but that I usually more or less keep to an hour. And that counseling with me has only two rules: that we speak our minds as freely and honestly as we can, and, second, that if I say anything that confuses or offends them or that seems to contradict their values or beliefs to please let me know at once.

"Tell me your story," I say, and then, "You know, I have to apologize, but I can be pretty dense and slow. So I want you to think of me as a kind of two year-old. Try and be as specific and concrete as you can, with plenty of examples. And try and tell it to me like a story, with lots of detail—tell me how it felt and what it looked like, if you can. A story, not a newspaper account."

The man starts off, but the woman corrects, fills in, and soon takes over the telling.

Six months ago the woman's sister was murdered by her boyfriend, beat to death after repeated episodes of physical abuse. Her seven year-old son, Bobby Joe, who is now eight and still fidgeting until I give him a handful of toy soldiers with which he starts to play, pitting them against each other in combat and adding sound effects, was asleep in the next room, or supposedly asleep. The boyfriend then took the boy to his mother's house who notified the police and told the child that her son had killed his mother. Child protective services took the child into care where he stayed, passing his birthday with a single foster parent, until my present clients decided to parent the child themselves and begin the adoption process. They have one older daughter who just graduated from high school and is taking a year off, working and living nearby in an apartment, before beginning college.

What's happening now as the child adjusts to this completely new situation, and as his new parents adjust to him, is escalating chaos. The parents are overwhelmed, angry, split, constantly on the verge of tears and fighting most of the time when they are not trying to deal with Bobby Joe. They speak of feeling powerless, feeling awful, vulnerable, almost out of control, subject to a rage they didn't know was in them, afraid of their own thoughts and fearful that they have made a dreadful mistake in taking this child into their home. He is too needy, won't mind, is at them constantly, whines, has temper tantrums in which he bites and scratches and breaks things, has gotten off to a terribly bad start with school which has just started.

The mother begins to cry. She loves the child. He needs a home, but right now she hates him. She says she thinks she's on the verge of a nervous breakdown. She hates herself. She just can't do it anymore. The husband tries to interject a note of optimism—but the woman turns on him. "I'm bearing the brunt of this" she says, "You're not home enough to know." He won't stay out of her bedroom. She can't even go to the bathroom without him knocking on the door or just coming in if she doesn't lock the door. He follows her around the house, asking constant questions. Aunt Joan, Aunt Joan, why, why, why?

Other than a few interjections intended to foster the flow of narrative and feelings, I've said very little during these first moments . . . but as they wind down and after a short silence in which I try to compose myself—my heart really has gone out to these people—it's not an unusual tale at all with children in need of families or placement . . . compose myself and compose in my mind what I want to say, I begin . . . "Wow, I really feel for you. I really do. It sounds totally overwhelming. It's like you were expecting someone to pull into your driveway but they slammed into your house, went through the garage, the kitchen, the living room, kept right on coming, now they've got you pinned in the bathroom and the engine still is revving.

"Well, I think we can get it turned off and backed up a little. There's hope. There really is. I've seen a lot of kids like this with major trauma, terrible losses and abuse, in their background. I saw a kid one time who accidentally shot and killed his father and was then left alone with the body in a room for a long, long time before someone found them. He came through, his family came through and so can you.

"Let me explain to you what's going on. But let me ask you first to imagine yourself in this situation, let's say that you have a job that you desperately need and you've heard layoffs are coming and you know that the meeting where who was going to be laid off would be decided was being held in an office directly in front of your desk.

"How do you think you'd feel while the meeting was going on? Do you think you'd be able to concentrate? Or do you think you'd be a basket case with your eyes fixed on that door, jumping out of your seat and skin every time that door opened with someone leaving to check their messages or just go to the bathroom. And let's imagine that the meeting goes on and on and that they break for lunch and you don't know whether the meeting's over and it's all decided or they're coming back.

"I think you'd go crazy. And I think during lunch you'd be pigeon-holing every person you could to see if they had heard anything. That 'heard anything, yet?' question would probably be asked a lot during the morning as people passed each other in the hall.

"What you'd be feeling is anxiety. It's a terribly uncomfortable feeling, maybe adaptive in some circumstances, but very uncomfortable. Your heart races, palpitates, your stomach gets queasy or jittery, you sweat, get clammy, tense, your mind ruminates, goes a mile a minute . . . what if . . . what if . . . what if . . . you ask yourself.

"That's what Bobby Joe is feeling, all the time, all . . . the time—though he doesn't know it, not precisely, not as you and I do, kids his age can't identify many feelings. It just feels good or bad inside, sort of like we adults taste things—we just like it, like it a lot, don't like it or don't like it a whole lot . . . and when they feel too bad, they act it out . . . they can't concentrate, can't sit still, get fidgety, ask a thousand questions . . . Have you heard anything . . . heard anything yet, so to speak. They get clingy, need your physical presence, need to see you, touch you, hear you, need you to constantly reassure them that you're there and alright.

"He's afraid of losing you the way he lost his mom." And then I turn to Bobby Joe, who's stopped fidgeting and is rapt with attention—Bobby Joe looks me in the eyes, looks me right in the eyes . . . "I'm sorry about your mother. Truly sorry. I think it's a horrible thing your step-dad did. I wish I could bring her back. I'm sorry it happened. I'm sorry he hurt you. And I'm sorry she died. I know you miss her so bad sometimes you just don't think you can stand it."

We're all crying a little now.

"Bobby Joe's afraid of losing you the way he lost his Mom—she was just there, then gone forever, no warning, nothing he could do about it, couldn't protect her, just snatched away. He won't leave you alone, can't get settled because he's afraid the same thing might happen to you and then to him again: loss too deep for tears, hurt so bad your heart, your soul just shuts down. It's hurt so big a child's heart just can't bear it.

"He needs two things from you right now, security and a way to identify his feelings and cope with them.

"Security, first, what you've got to remember about kids is that they feel secure, which is their basic psychological need, only when they believe their parents are in control and know what they're doing. They're like passengers on a plane. If they're flying through rough weather they don't want to see the pilot out of control or coming back into the cabin to ask them what they think or how they feel about what's happening.

"What I want you to do this morning"—and here I rely on some other details they've provided. They, like many parents, get their kids up way too early in the mornings and spend the rest of the time before leaving in a frustrating verbal battle struggling to hurry them up—make them eat breakfast, brush their teeth, get dressed.

"I don't want you to get Bobby up until you're completely ready and there's just enough time for him to get ready if he does it double time. I want you to come quietly into his bedroom with a glass of orange juice in your hand. Wake him gently—after a couple days of this he'll be waiting for you. Give him your undivided attention. Pretend like you're a couple of valets whose job it is to get the gentleman ready. Buy a John Phillips Sousa CD and play it, get him to drink the orange juice and then hustle him through what he needs to do. And if it goes off without a hitch have a little surprise treat ready for him in the car. It will get the day off to a good start. He'll love it and it will show him you're in charge. It will relieve some of his anxiety. Don't worry, I only ask you to do this for one week. Breaks the cycle, then, we'll see what happens.

"You got to do it. You've got to focus on it. Getting back in control of kids is like fighting a land war where you advance foot by foot. But once you've taken some ground, you can't give it back or you not only lose ground, you lose confidence and the kid sees you can be beaten. You can't do it half-way. If you do you're going to get pushed back into the sea and drown.

"Second, I want you to sit down with him, both of you, with manila paper, glitter, scissors, glue, crayons, magazines, and a dictionary. Look up the word anxiety and in the center of the paper have Bobby write it out. Draw some funny faces around it. Pick one of them and name him Mr. Anxiety. Write down twenty questions coming out of his mouth . . . Why? Why? Why? Put it on the refrigerator and then this week, three times and three times only, when Bobby really seems to be struggling, get down on your knees, grasp him by the shoulders, look him right in the eyes, and tell him you're sorry he is feeling so bad inside. Maybe he's feeling anxious, or scared or sad. Give him a big bear hug, tell him you love him and ask him to go look at the refrigerator."

I try to reinforce my directives by saying that sometimes I feel like a physician. A patient calls and says, "Doc, I got a headache," I say, "take two aspirins and call me in the morning." Then they call back at 2 a.m. and say, "Doc I've still got the headache." I say, "Did you take the aspirin?" They say, "Well no, I was kind of hoping it would go away on its own." At that point, I have to wonder whose fault it is that they've still got this headache.

Then a few words to prepare for next week. "While you're getting him ready and when you make the picture and ask him to look at, please pay close attention to what's happening, to what everybody's saying and doing and feeling. We'll focus on that next week. This will not only help ya'll, it will give us something productive to focus on and talk about so we can build some momentum."

Family Preservation

> There are in my own country families who for centuries have
> lived under the influence of a motto; I have known members
> of several generations of them and have found them to vary in
> many ways, but the stamp has been recognizable in each of them,
> and the people who have lived under the sign of *Nobilis est ira*
> *leonis* will differ in countenance and even in instincts from those
> under *Amore non vi.*
>
> —Isak Dinesen, *Daguerreotypes*

I've been asked what I think about adoption, about intra-family adoption, about guardianship, about family preservation.

I think it possible to make a strong moral-philosophical—but fundamentally spiritual argument that "preserving families in a culture of life" is nearly always (I mean this as a principal, not an ideology) the right thing to do when a mother and father and the extended kin and family are experiencing the crisis of how to care for a child: perhaps an unexpected child, perhaps even, initially, while in the midst of panic, confusion and shame, "unwanted." By "right" I mean a position that speaks to people at the level of their basic needs, ideals and beliefs—the need to feel respected, to be free, safe, to think well of one's self and be thought of as decent by others; the ideals of love and loyalty, of continuity and connection, of kinship, of carrying on, whether the Holy Family fleeing to Egypt as the result of Joseph's dream, or Aeneas abandoning burning Troy with his father clasping his back while in his arms sheltering his household gods. I think it possible to elevate the discourse, to inspire and unite people in this way, to a vision of what is truly possible for them. This is simply a vision that would piercingly and persuasively remind people—espe-

cially, but not, of course, exclusively, people of Faith, on the basis
of their most deeply held religious convictions, (but aren't all of us
somehow religious in this way, believers in what Faulkner called "the
old verities," T.S. Eliot, "the permanent things," and Yeats, "the Presences that passion, piety or affection knows" or even Lincoln, "the
better angel of our nature")—of the grandeur and scope and necessary reach of the human spirit. I think it possible as well to inspire
people, locally, regionally, nationally, globally, to extend a helping
hand, to provide emotional support, material assistance, to embody
and promulgate an attitude that fosters hope and dignity to parents
and families unnerved and reeling in the face of such crisis and need.
I also believe, and, hope that it is an idea whose time, by rights and of
necessity, has come.

But such a view requires tribunes, voices, authorities, and a coher-
ent vision of what is right, fair, decent, and beautiful and astonishing to observe and experience when this vision of families preserved,
clinging to each other, supporting each other, sharing joy and pain
and tragedy, tears and laughter and grace, struggling to get by, filled
with doubt and dread of the future as so many families are today, upholding (dare I say it) the family's honor in the sense of that extraordinary Catholic writer Georges Bernanos (see his magnificent *Diary
of a Country Priest*)—upholding honor and holding and cradling a
child, is realized and fulfilled. This is a work that needs to be done.
This is a work that I, together with many, many others, am trying to
do, as a counselor, as a family therapist, as a writer, and as a man.
It must be done. As I read this morning on the marquee at the local
Baptist Church: "Let's love our children—that will teach them."

REFLECTIONS

The poet's voice need not merely be the record of man, it can be one of the props, the pillars, to help him endure and prevail.
—William Faulkner, Nobel Prize Speech

What are you trying to do? What is the purpose of all this? And what would I like to see more of in the traditions that have nurtured me, the fields in which I've practiced—adoption and child welfare; the practice of counseling and family therapy and the discipline of psychology?

What I try to do is speak . . . what I try to do is speak a language, a language of truth

and goodness and beauty

and honor

that inspires and uplifts,

that brings out the best in people, that inspires them to

reconnect to their core beliefs and virtues, to the springs of their compassion,

to the strength of their courage, to the wisdom of their common sense.

To keep faith with all that is best in them.

When I attempt to do this, I remember Churchill: "The Oxford philosopher Isaiah Berlin remarked that Churchill 'idealized' his countrymen 'with such intensity that in the end they approached his ideal and began to see themselves as he saw them.'" and MacArthur, Kennedy, King, President Obama.

I remember "Christendom's Troubadour," Frederick D. Wilhelmsen, who scrawled atop my first exam in Metaphysics "Bloody good"

I remember Bernanos and the Curé de Torcy

I remember preachers

I remember Richard Weaver's insistence that "all language is sermonic"

I remember Faulkner and Yeats

I remember Robert Louis Stevenson's: "It is the history of kindnesses that alone makes this world tolerable. If it were not for that, for the effect of kind words, kind looks, kind letters, multiplying, spreading, making one happy through another and bringing forth benefits, some fifty, some a thousand fold, I should be tempted to think our life a practical jest in the worst possible spirit."

I remember the Beatitudes, the Golden Rule, and John 3:16 and I remember St. Paul's exhortation to "fight the good fight," "to run the race" and to put on the "armor of Faith" and I remember that "the greatest of these is love."

It would be a powerful rhetoric, one weighty and luminous, one that displays Tillich's "courage to be" and Wilhelmsen's "courage to be a part;" it would speak as an "I to a Thou" in Buber's sense, and see the world and our participation in it not as a problem to be solved but as a mystery to be revered and explored with an attitude of wonder (Gabriel Marcel).

I am trying to establish a genre of honor, a rhetoric and a therapy that is true to and keeps faith with the "old verities," the best in humanity, in myself and in the people with whom I speak. Of course, I fail in this, more often than not, but it is worth the effort, an effort that tries to remember and reach out, that tries to praise and give thanks, that tries to be kind and to help. I have made this effort throughout my career and I will sustain it.

A Creed

Stand erect, hold your heads high, because your Liberation is
near at hand.

—Luke 21:28

to believe and believe in people
to hurt with those in pain
to comfort those who need comforting
to focus on positives and strengths
to speak an inspirational language

to be a heartening voice
that revives and strengthens

to be life-guide
truth-sayer
voice of experience
calm in the storm

to live, serve and practice
with honor

CODA

JAMES HILLMAN: AN APPRECIATION

I knew James Hillman. For a time, during my twenties, I worked for him at Spring Publications. My memory, where Hermes must lurk now, since my memory is constantly playing tricks on me, adds I was also his graduate assistant when he was Graduate Dean at the University of Dallas. The first position blended with the second and with several other roles, not the least of which was the "lucky to get to do it" duty of regular chauffeur.

I knew him to be a very gracious and generous man—a real, though casual and understated, Old World Gentleman, if I might use that term. He was certainly kind to me and tolerant of a variety of contretemps, more tolerant than I would have been, which I can say with some authority, having reached the age that he was when I knew him.

But to say much more about a "personal" relationship, fanciful or not, with "J.H." would be to miss the point, the entirely gratuitously-bestowed-on-me good fortune of knowing James Hillman and of knowing his work inside and out, because that is what and who he ultimately is: his work, his oeuvre, his opus. To know him meant to work with him, to be a companion along the way. As I have suggested, he was a boon companion. Belloc said, "A man is more himself if he is one of a number," which was undoubtedly true with Hillman. This is why I never thought of Hillman as Jungian in his personal demeanor; he was much more Adlerian: the versatile chef, the gracious host, with a good-humored chuckle and easy laughter, eminently companionable. But the companionship, the knack for friendship, the ostensibly effortless and evidently unselfconscious and certainly

un-self-important mentoring that came so naturally to him was secondary, almost a byproduct, of the work. He could be testy, irascible,
stubborn, myopic, but never petty or mean. His hatreds were intellectual. I never knew him to hold a grudge or even to speak unflatter-
ingly of those whose envy or enmity, almost apoplectic at times and
nearly always excessive, harassed and sought to anathematize him.
For Hillman foils were welcome if they challenged him to a greater
precision in his thought; and fools not completely unforgiveable.

What a magnificent work it is! Hillman recovered soul to psychology, which to my mind is to say that he recovered psychology for
an age—mid- to late-twentieth century, the age from MacNamara to
the neo-cons, from Volcker to Greenspan, from RET to the kinder,
gentler CBT, the age in psychology of the atavistic Boulder conference and statement (just when, with the principle of indeterminancy,
physics transcended the Newtonian "scientific" model, psychology
embraced it!)—nearly bereft of it.

Some say he built on Jung. I wonder. Jungianism, as I experienced
it, which was, admittedly, at the margins, was a Church. As Churches
go, it was tolerable. Jung allowed secular, liberal, Protestants, including ex-ministers and seminary dropouts, to become imitation Catholics, almost medieval Catholics (which is what I count myself to be)
with a sacred rite (analysis), devotional practices (active imagination
and dreamwork,) even Saints (the little people of the psyche), and, of
course, a Pope, and, then, a canonized Pope, who was Jung himself.
Notwithstanding several entertaining books, I don't think Jung ever
went beyond that; he was too much the analytical psychologist and
earthy Swiss to believe himself "the Aryan Christ."

Since I was and remain a Catholic, practicing, believing, although
the Jungian enchantments were strong, the allure was finally un-
satisfying. It was Merlin's glimmering, shimmering magic, not the

sensual-spiritual comforts and historical continuity of the Sacramental Mass.

I'll leave it to Jungians and the Church—as Lenny Bruce used
to say, the Catholic Church is the only "The" Church—to define
soul in the religious sense. It is to Hillman that I give the credit, the
honor, of recovering the soul as psychological; that is, he restored
the soul to the world, to being in the world, to the world as the vale
of soul-making.

Hillman made psychology worldly again. If that had not sufficed
for me, and it did, in Hillman there were intimations of other familiar personal loves and loyalties: chivalry, for example, "Oh air, pride
plume here Buckle" and of the psychologist not as scientific practitioner, neutral observer, witness or wizard, but as Knight Errant. In
Suicide and the Soul he spoke of the classical, chivalric virtue of courage, of psychological courage, of the courage to stand for the soul's
deep, deep wounds as critical to soul-making. Further, everything in
Hillman teems with history, of history as present and meaningful, of
the present as shot through with what happened when the Emperor
Julian died, or Justinian closed the schools, or the Church Fathers
met in Council, or Petrarch climbed Mont Ventoux in April 1336 or
when Patton's tanks rolled across the Rhineland. Somewhere Hillman says "I will ride that Horse of History until I drop." In his latest
book, *A Terrible Love of War*, the index cites Patton more than Jung.
Blood and guts and action in the world have become as valuable and
significant as memories, dreams and reflections.

How could Hillman not appeal, with a force like a gale, to a young
psychologist, myself, starting to make his own way in the world, afire
with his own incipient vision, a vision of psychology and analysis
that I would come to call "spiritual existentialism," a Catholic, worldly, poetic-strategic psychology of chivalry and courage, an approach

whose goal for readers and patients is "a worldly wisdom that becomes a force for good"?

How could this body of work, with the sweep of its scholarship,
the dazzle of its style, the astonishing subtlety and nuance it dis-
played about the twists and turns of psychological life, not arrest and
compel me? *Revisioning Psychology* did this to me, for me, in a powerful effect only heightened and broadened by thirty years of devotedly
reading Hillman.

I have not seen or talked to or heard from Hillman for over a quarter of a century, which is probably best, as I don't think I would ever
have done my own work if I'd not veered off to resume the road that
I flatter myself I was already on when I met him.

But if I might purloin at least the ingredients of a metaphor, I'll
close by saying that Hillman remains in my pantheon of heroes. In
Revisioning Psychology, Hillman commemorates the Renaissance
practice of engaging "in imaginative discourse with persons of antiquity. Petrarch wrote long letters to his inner familiars, Livy, Vergil,
Seneca, Cicero, Horace, and sent regards to Homer and Hesiod. Erasmus prayed to divine Socrates . . . Machiavelli sought solace in the
company of ancient heroes, poets and legendary figures . . . " If books
may be said to serve as spirits, then in my study and imaginative
discourse *Revisioning Psychology* shares pride of place with Haley's
Uncommon Therapy, Belloc's *The Four Men*, and Frederick D. Wilhelmsen's *The Metaphysics of Love*. For me, *Revisioning Psychology*,
together with all of Hillman's other books, together with a few years
of personal contact as in "I knew him when and reasonably well"
as a student knows his teacher, has been an irreplaceable guide, an
inexhaustible source, an inspiring, sometimes infuriating, but always
challenging companion along the way. Peace be to its author and
blessings on his head.

NOTES

1   Jung, *Symbols of Transformation*, 338, 228.

2   Jaspers, *General Psychopathology*, 334.

3   See Hillman, *Revisioning Psychology*.

4   Hillman, *Loose Ends*, 142.

5   Hillman, *Emotion*, 16.

6   James Lehrberger, "Christendom's Troubadour" in *The Intercollegiate Review*, Spring, 1999, 52-55.

7   Wilhelmsen, *Citizen of Rome*, 118.

8   Ibid., 162.

9   See Miller, *The New Polytheism: Rebirth of the Gods and Goddesses*.

10   See Moore, *The Care of the Soul: A Guide for Cultivating Depth and Sacredness in Everyday Life*.

11   See Samuels, *Jung and the Post-Jungians*.

12   Berry, *Echo's Subtle Body*, 153, 154. This entire book is decisive for practice. Especially valuable is "Rules of Thumb Toward an Archetypal Psychology Practice," which, in my view, serves as a bridge both into and out of Hillman and into a tradition for which Hillman's body of work provides orientation, inspiration, challenge but is in no way a sacred text or confining orthodoxy. As Hillman himself has said: "There is not one archetypal psychology; there are many archetypal psychologies."

13   Cochrane, *Christianity and Classical Culture*, 31-32.

14   Johannesson, *The Renaissance of the Goths in Sixteenth Century Sweden*, 92.

15   Hart, *Viscount Bolingbroke: Tory Humanist*, 152.

16   Kaiser Wolfram, *Christian Democracy and the Origins of European Union*.

17   Tate, *Essays of Four Decades*, 576.

18   Gomez Davila, "The Authentic Reactionary" in *Modern Age*, 80.

Reactionary here is a psychological rather than political notion. Belloc writes, "The bulk of men will accept an event, unless it be quite outrageously opposed to their daily habits. Further the bulk of men are moved by tradition and custom and nearly always incline, very vaguely, to a continuance of what they have known. And at the same time, paradoxically, all men have an appetite for something new and are more or less adventurous for a change." (Hilaire Belloc, *The Cruise of the Nona, Penguin*, 1925, pp. 140-141.) This is right. Most of us by nature are conservatives. As Oakeshotte noted, the psychological basis for conservativism is a fear of loss, of things known and loved, familiar and tangible being stolen or slipping away. At the same time, paradoxically, we are by nature progressives; we all crave "the shock of the new"; are "adventurous for a change." Here, from a psychological point of view, the High Modernists of "the Pound Era," Pound, Eliot, Lewis, the Fugitives John Crowe Ransom and Allen Tate, are the better guides together with the High Modernism that ultimately crested with Marshall McLuhan, a Catholic Chestertonian who remains the keenest exegete of present day times. (Marshall McLuhan and Frederick Wilhelmsen, who collaborated and shared a close friendship, were, in many ways, though never self-identified nor self-realized as such, the ChesterBelloc of the mid-twentieth century.) The "reactionary temperament" is at times conservative and at times progressive but normatively steers through life according to Hillman's "aesthetic reflex," that is, the instinctive, considered responses that are "the thought of the heart" and once went by the name of virtue, that is, prudence emboldened by fortitude, secured by temperance and anchored in the justice that accords realities their due. As Belloc suggests, it is usually only outrage that causes the stubborn cleaving to or sudden change of course that, in the life of a man or a nation,, ultimately proves determining.

19   Hillman, *The Thought of the Heart and The Soul of the World*, 66.

20   Wilhelmsen, *Citizen of Rome*, 311.

21   Tate, op. cit., 304.

22   Adler, *Superiority and Social Interest, A Collection of Later Writings*, 200.

To connect Adler to Rome on the evidence of his name is without question an "equestrian leap" (Lorca) of the imagination. It is the sort of leap characteristically taken by Hillman and in the practice of an archetypal psychology grounded in a poetic basis of mind. The leap itself is paradigmatic and requires no other justification.

Nevertheless, the horse lands somewhere. The value of archetypal psychology is that these landings are so illuminating in what they produce. Adler's psychology is clearly a Roman psychology. Adler's "social interest" corresponds with Vico's *sensus communis*. As Gadamer indicates: "According to Vico, what gives the human will its direction is not the abstract universality of reason but the concrete universality represented by the community of a group, a people, a nation, or the whole human race. Hence developing the communal sense is of decisive importance for living." (Gadamer, p. 19.) And " . . . Vico goes back to the old Roman concept of the *sensus communis*, as found especially in the Roman classics which, when faced with Greek cultivation, held firmly to the value and significance of their own traditions of civil and social life. A critical note directed against the theoretical speculations of the philosophers can be heard in the Roman concept of the *sensus communis . . .* " (Gadamer, p. 20.) In this brief explanation resides my view of Adler and hence the basis for my "Adlerian," Roman, practice of archetypal psychology.

23   Onians, *Origins of European Thought*, 166, 167.

24   Sturlson, *Heimskringla: History of the Kings of Norway*, tr. Lee M. Hollander, 516.

25   Wilhelmsen, *Man's Knowledge of Reality: An Introduction of Thomistic Epistemology*, 100.

26   Manchester, *American Caesar*, 15, 18, 19.

27   Ortega y Gasset, *What is Philosophy?*, 119, 120.

28   Ibid., 120.

29   Bachelard, *Air and Dreams: An Essay on the Imagination of Movement*, 153-154

30   Belloc, *Paris*, 276, 277.

31   Nietzsche, *The Gay Science*, 318.

32   Gellius, quoted in *Religions of Rome: A Sourcebook*, Vol. II, ed. Mary Beard, et. al., 217.

33   Hart, *Scipio Africanus: Greater than Napoleon*, 273, 241, *vi*.

34   See Cochrane, 122, Warde Fowler, *Roman Ideas of Deity*, 1914.

35   Wilhelmsen, *The Paradoxicial Structure of Existence*, 157.

36   Olson, *Call Me Ishmael*, 57.

37   Belloc, *William the Conqueror*, 52-53.

38   Duby, *William Marshall: The Flower of Chivalry*, 20.

39   Lukacs, *Churchill: Visionary. Statesman. Historian.*, 175.

40   Ibid, 171.

41   Kaplan, *Warrior Politics.*

42   Pieper, *Guide to Thomas Aquinas*, 45-46.

43   von Balthasar, *Tragedy Under Grace: Reinhold Schneider on the Experience of the West,* 247, 251.

44   Burchardt, *The Civilization of the Renaissance in Italy*, 91.

45   Kelly, *Eleanor of Aquitaine*, 167.

46   Bottome, *Alfred Adler*, 19.

47   McLynn, *Robert Louis Stevenson: A Biography*, 514.

48   Chesterton, *Saint Thomas Aquinas*, 7, 8, 9.

49   Ibid., 5.

50   Lenkeith, *Dante and the Legend of Rome*, 173.

51   Ibid., 164.

52   Ibid., 170-171.

53   Dante, *La Vita Nuova*, tr. Barbara Reynolds, 54.

54   Wilhelmsen, *The Metaphysics of Love*, 153.

55   Wilhelmsen, *Being and Knowing*, 282.

56   van Deursen, *Everyday Mysteries*, 161.

57   Kaplan, op. cit., 17.

58   Haley, *Uncommon Therapy*, 234, 204.

59   Haley, *The Milton H. Erickson Foundation Newsletter*, Vol. 27, No. 2., 23-24.

60   Patton, *The Pattons*, 378.

61   Manchester, op. cit., 401.

62   Alter, *The Defining Moment*, 63, 215, 216.

63   Williams, *The Last Great Frenchman: A Life of General de Gaulle*, 345.

64   Cloud and Jaffe, *The Fourth Star*, 145.

65   This description is by a Northern journalist after Appomattox. Lee was always described as a "A man of considerable handsomeness and moral grandeur . . . " (p. 128, *The Civil War: A Narrative*, Shelby Foote, Random House, 1958).

While still a young man, at West Point, he was called the "Marble Model." " . . . he was tall for his time, five feet, eleven inches, and he was incredibly handsome. Lee adopted a military bearing and posture without becoming even slightly stiff, and he moved with grace and poise. His eyes were dark brown, sharp and engaging; his black hair waved and was thick and full." (Emory Thomas, p. 54.) At age fifty-four a staff officer recalled him "Admirably proportioned, of graceful and dignified carriage, with strikingly handsome features, bright and penetrating eyes, his iron-gray hair closely cut, his face cleanly shaved except for a mustache, he appeared every inch a soldier and a man born to command." (Thomas, p. 192.)

66 Chalmers, "Forrest and his Campaigns," in Brock *Southern Historical Society Papers*, Vol. VII, 1879, No. 10.

67 Harris, *Imperium*, 72.

68 Luttwak, *The Grand Strategy of the Byzantine Empire*, 7

69 Puzo, *The Last Don*, 61.

70 Hillman, *A Terrible Love of War*, 36.

71 D'Este, *Warlord: A Life of Winston Churchill at War*, 481.

72 Manchester, op. cit., 468.

73 Brown, *Apocalypse And/Or Metamorphosis*, 190.

74 See Kugelmann, *The Windows of Soul: Psychological Physiology of the Human Eye and Primary Glaucoma.*

75 Kurosawa, *Something Like an Autobiography*, Knopf, 95, 192.

76 Neumann, "Engels and Marx: Military Concepts of the Social Revolutionaries," in *Makers of Modern Strategy*, ed. Edward Mead Earl.

77 Leclercq, *The Love of Learning and the Desire for God*, 132-133.

78 Fall, *Hell In A Very Small Place: The Siege of Dien Bien Phu*, 51.

79 Ibid., 51-52.

80 Fuller "The Reformation of War," quoted in Hart, op. cit., 267.

81 Minuchin and Fishman, *Family Therapy Techniques*, 29.

82 Fisch, Weakland, Segal, *The Tactics of Change*, 22.

83 Minuchin, *Mastering Family Therapy*, 38.

84 Wilhelmsen, *Citizen of Rome*, 312.

85 Gilson, *The Christian Philosophy of St. Thomas Aquinas*, 373.

86 Walker, *Rhetoric and Poetics in Antiquity*, 9.

87 Manchester, op. cit., 835.

88 Johannesson, op. cit., 38-39.

89 Furtmüller, "Alfred Adler: A Biographical Essay" in Adler, 358-359.

90 Nietzsche, op. cit., 254.

91 Gadamer, *Truth and Method*, 15.

92 Hillman, "The Feeling Function" in *Jung's Typology*, 144.

93 Ibid., 141, 142.

94 *The Song of Roland*, tr. W.S. Merwin, 6.

95 Sperber, *The Masks of Loneliness: Alfred Adler in Perspective*, XIV.

96 Grassi, *Rhetoric as Philosophy: The Humanist Tradition*, 45.

97 Taylor, *An American Soldier: The Wars of General Maxwell Taylor*, 400, Appendix A, "Leading the American Soldier" by Maxwell Taylor.

98 Perret, *Old Soldiers Never Die*, 360.

99 Lévy, *American Vertigo*, 176-177.

100 Tate, op. cit., 570.

101 Faulkner, *Absalom, Absalom*, 111-112.

102 Pettigru, *Notes on Spain and the Spaniards*, xiii.

103 Ibid., 430.

104 Ibid., 18.

105 Norwich, *The Other Conquest*, 331.

106 Kaplan, *Mediterranean Winter*, 113.

107 Wilson, *Hilaire Belloc*, 379.

108 Belloc, *Hills and the Sea*, 42.

109 Sword, *Southern Invincibility*, 30.

110 Wilhelmsen, "Hilaire Belloc: Defender of the Faith" in McInerny, *The Catholic Writer*, 1989, 85.

111 Allitt, *Catholic Intellectuals and Conservative Politics in America, 1950-1985*, 145-146. All the indexed entries regarding Wilhelmsen are valuable.

112 Olson, op.cit., 73.

113 Lytle, *Kristin*, 51.

114 Ibid., 54.

115 Quoted in *Brave New Family: G.K. Chesterton on Men and Women, Children, Sex, Divorce, Marriage & the Family*, edited by De Silva, 12.

116 Taylor, op. cit., 398.

117 Gadamer, op. cit., 320.

118 Lukacs, *The Duel: The Eighty-Day Struggle Between Churchill and Hitler*, 43.

119 Perret, op. cit.,191.

120 Remini, *Andrew Jackson, Vol. I*, 8.

121 Tate, op. cit., 583.

122 Malone, *Jefferson: The Sage of Monticello*, 192, 193.

123 Severson, *Spiritual Existential Counseling*, 44, 45.

124 Wilhelmsen, *The Metaphysics of Love*, 32.

125 von Balthazar, *Bernanos*, 563.

126 Rahner, *The Spirituality of St. Ignatius Loyola*, 15.

127 von Balthasar, *The Grain of Wheat: Aphorisms*, 65.

128 Jackson, *The Care of the Psyche*, 28.

129 Bernanos, *Diary of a Country Priest*, 17.

130 Ellenberger, *The Discovery of the Unconscious: The History and Evolution of Dynamic Psychiatry*, 609.

131 Severson, *Prose/Poems*, private printing.

132 Merleau-Ponty, *The Phenomenology of Perception*, 530n.

133 Belloc, *Hills and the Sea*, 255.

134 Gilson, op.cit., 292.

135 Thomas, *Robert Kennedy: His Life*, 286.

136 Gilson, op.cit., 287, 288.

137 Ellenberger, op.cit., 609.

138 Furtmüller, *Alfred Adler: A Biographical Essay*, in Adler, op.cit., 309.

139 Bonhoeffer, *Dietrich Bonhoeffer: Writings Selected by Robert Coles*, 118.

140 Wilhelmsen, *Citizen of Rome*, 312.

Sources Cited

Adler, Alfred. *Superiority and Social Interest*, ed. Heinz and Rowena Ansbacher. Norton, 1979.

Allitt, Patrick. *Catholic Intellectuals and Conservative Politics in America, 1950-1985*. Cornell University Press, 1993.

Alter, Jonathan. *The Defining Moment*. Simon and Schuster, 2006.

Bachelard, Gaston. *Air and Dreams: An Essay on the Imagination of Movement*. Dallas Institute Publications, Dallas Institute of Humanities and Culture, 1988.

Beard, Mary, John North, Simon Price. *Religions of Rome: Volume 2, A Sourcebook*. Cambridge University Press, 1998.

Belloc, Hilaire.
- *The Cruise of the Nona*. Houghton Mifflin Company, 1925.
- *Europe and the Faith*. The Paulist Press, 1920.
- *The Four Men*. Nelson and Sons, 1912.
- *Hills and the Sea*. Scribner's, 1906.
- *Paris*. Metheun, 1900.
- *William the Conqueror*. Tan, 1992.

Georges Bernanos. *Diary of a Country Priest*. Macmillan Company, 1937.

Berry, Patricia. *Echo's Subtle Body*. Spring, 2008.

Bloom, Harold, ed. *Romanticism and Consciousness*. W.W. Norton, 1970.

Blumenson, Martin. *The Patton Papers 1885-1940*. Houghton Mifflin, 1972.

Boardman, John, ed. *The Oxford History of the Roman World*. Oxford, 1986.

Bonhoeffer, Dietrich. *Dietrich Bonhoeffer: Writings Selected by Robert Coles*. Orbis Books, 1998.

Bottome, Phyllis. *Alfred Adler*. G.P. Putnam's Sons, 1939.

Brock, Robert Alonzo. *Southern Historical Society Papers, Volume 7*. Broadfoot Publishing Company, Morningside Bookshop, 1879.

Brown, Norman O. *Apocalypse And/Or Metamorphosis*. University of California Press, 1992.

Burckhardt, Jacob. *The Civilization of Renaissance In Italy*. Penguin, 1990.

Chesterton, G.K.
– *Saint Thomas Aquinas*. San Torode, 2010.
– *The Ballad of the White Horse*. Methuen, 1911.

Cloud, David and Greg Jaffe. *The Fourth Star*. Crown, 2009.

Cochrane, Charles Norris. *Christianity and Classical Culture*. Oxford, 1964.

Dante.
– *La Vita Nuova*. tr. Barbara Reynolds. Penguin, 1969.
– *The Divine Comedy*. tr. James Finn Cotter. Stonybrook, 2006.

Davila, Nicolas Gomez. "The Authentic Reactionary" in *Modern Age*, Vol. 52, No. 1. Winter, 2010.

D'Este Carlo.
– *A Genius for War*. Harper Collins, 1995.
– *Warlord: A Life of Winston Churchill at War*. Harper, 2008.

De Silva, Alvaro. *Brave New Family: G.K. Chesterton on Men and Women, Children, Sex, Divorce, Marriage & the Family*. Ignatius Press, 1990.

Duby, Georges. *William Marshall*. Pantheon, 1985.

Ellenberger, Henri F. *The Discovery of the Unconscious: The History and Evolution of Dynamic Psychiatry*. Basic Books, 2008.

Fall, Bernard B. *Hell in a Very Small Place: The Siege of Dien Bien Phu*. Da Capo, 2002.

Faulkner, William. *Absalom, Absalom*. Vintage, 1986.

Fisch, Richard, John H. Weakland, and Lynn Segal. *The Tactics of Change*. Josey-Bass, 1983.

Foote, Shelby. *The Civil War: A Narrative*. Random House, 1958.

Fuller, J. F. C. *Reformation of War, Part 1*. BiblioBazaar, 2013.

Gadamer, Hans-Georg. *Truth and Method*. Continuum, 1975.

Gilson, Etienne. *The Christian Philosophy of St. Thomas Aquinas*. Norte Dame Press, 1994.

Grassi, Ernesto. *Rhetoric as Philosophy: The Humanist Tradition*. Pennsylvania State University Press, 1980.

Haley, Jay.
– *Uncommon Therapy*. W.W. Norton, 1973.
– *The Milton H. Erickson Foundation Newsletter*, Vol. 27, No.2.

Harris, Robert. *Imperium*. Simon and Schuster, 2006.

Hart, B.H. Liddell. *Scipio Africanus: Greater Than Napoleon*. Da Capo Press, 2004.

Hart, Jeffrey. *Viscount Bolingbroke: Tory Humanist*. Routledge, 1965.

Hillman, James.
– *Emotion*. Routledge & Kegan Paul, 1960.
– *Jung's Typology*. Spring, 1984.
– *The Myth of Analysis*. Northwestern, 1972.
– *Revisioning Psychology*. Harper, 1975.

– *Suicide and the Soul*. Spring, 1964.

– *A Terrible Love of War*. Penguin, 2004.

– *The Thought of the Heart and The Soul of the World*. Spring, 1981.

– "Why Archetypal Psychology?" *Loose Ends*. Spring, 1975.

Hopkins, Gerard Manley. *Poems and Prose*. Penguin, 1953.

Jackson, Stanley. *The Care of the Psyche*. Yale University Press, 1997.

Jaspers, Karl. *General Psychopathology*. University of Chicago Press, 1964.

Johannesson, Kurt. *The Renaissance of the Goths in Sixteenth Century Sweden*. University of California, 1982.

Jung, C.G. *Symbols of Transformation*. Princeton University Press, 1956.

Kaiser, Wolfram. *Christian Democracy and the Origins of European Union*. Cambridge University Press, 2007.

Kaplan, Robert D.

– *Mediterranean Winter*. Random House, 2011.

– *Warrior Politics*. Random House, 2002.

Kelly, Amy. *Eleanor of Aquitaine*. Harvard, 1950.

Kugelmann, Robert. *The Windows of Soul: Psychological Physiology of the Human Eye and Primary Glaucoma*. Bucknell University Press, 1983.

Kurosawa, Akira. *Something Like An Autobiography*. Random House, 2011.

Leclercq, Jean. *The Love of Learning and the Desire for God*. Fordham, 1961.

Lehrberger, James, O. Cist. "Christendom's Troubadour: Frederick D. Wilhelmsen". *The Intercollegiate Review*. Spring, 1996.

Lenkeith, Nancy. *Dante and the Legend of Rome*. The Warburg Institute, 1952.

Lévy, Bernard Henry-Levy. *American Vertigo*. Random House, 2007.

Lukacs, John.
– *Churchill: Visionary. Statesman. Historian.* Yale University Press, 2004.
– *The Duel: The Eighty-Day Struggle Between Churchill and Hitler.* Yale University Press, 2001.

Luttwak, Edward N. *The Grand Strategy of the Byzantine Empire*. Harvard University Press, 2009.

Lytle, Andrew. *Kristin*. University of Missouri Press, 1992.

Malone, Dumas. *Jefferson The Sage of Monticello*. Little Brown and Company, 1977.

Manchester, William. *American Caesar*. Dell, 1978.

McCarthy, Cormac. *No Country for Old Men*. Knopf, 2005.

McInerny, Ralph M., Wethersfield Institute. *The Catholic Writer*. Ignatius Press, 1991.

McLuhan, Marshall. *The Interior Landscape: the Literary Criticism of Marshall McLuhan*. McGraw Hill, 1971.

McLynn, Frank. *Robert Louis Stevenson: A Biography*. Random House, 1993

Merleau-Ponty, Maurice. *Phenomenology of Perception*. Routledge, 2013.

Miller, David L. *The New Polytheism; Rebirth of the Gods and Goddesses*. Harper & Row, 1974.

Minuchin, Salvador. *Mastering Family Therapy*. John Wiley and Sons, 1996.

Minuchin, Salvador, and H.C. Fishman. *Family Therapy Techniques*. Harvard, 1981.

Moore, Thomas. *Care of the Soul: A Guide for Cultivating Depth and Sacredness in Everyday Life*. HarperPerennial, 1994.

Nietzsche, Friedrich. *The Gay Science*. Vintage, 1974.

Neumann, Sigmund. "Engels and Marx: Military Concepts of the Social Revolutionaries," in *Makers of Modern Strategy*. ed. Edward Mead Earle. Princeton University Press, 1943.

Norwich, John Julius. *The Other Conquest*. Harper & Row, 1967.

Olson, Charles. *Call Me Ishmael*. Johns Hopkins, 1997.

Onians, Richard. *The Origins of European Thought*. Cambridge, 1954.

Ortega y Gasset, José. *What is Philosophy?* W.W. Norton, 1960.

Patton, Robert H. *The Pattons*. Crown, 1994.

Pettigru, James Johnston. *Notes on Spain and the Spaniards*. University of South Carolina Press, 2010.

Perret, Geoffrey. *Old Soldiers Never Die*. Random House, 1996.

Phares, Ross. *Cavalier in the Wilderness*. Pelican, 1998.

Pieper, Josef. *Guide to Thomas Aquinas*. Ignatius Press, 1991.

Puzo, Mario. *The Last Don*. Random House, 2004.

Rahner, Karl. *Ignatius of Loyola*. HarperCollins Publishers Limited, 1979

Remini, Robert V. *Andrew Jackson, Volume I*. The Johns Hopkins University Press, 1977.

Samuels, Andrew. *Jung and the Post-Jungians*. Routledge, 1986.

Severson, Randolph. *Spiritual Existential Counseling*. Boscobel, 1999.

Shaara, Jeff. *Rise to Rebellion*. Ballantine, 2001.

Sperber, Manes. *Masks of Loneliness: Alfred Adler in Perspective*. Macmillian, 1974.

Sturluson, Snorri. tr. Lee M. Hollander, *Heimskringla History of the Kings of Norway*. University of Texas, 1964.

Sword, Wiley. *Southern Invincibility*. St. Martin's Press, 1999.

Tate, Allen. *Essays of Four Decades*. ISI Books, 1999.

Taylor, John M. *An American Soldier: The Wars of General Maxwell Taylor*. Presidio, 1989.

Thomas, Emory M. *Robert E. Lee: A Biography*. W. W. Norton & Company, 1997.

Thomas, Evan. *Robert Kennedy: His Life*. Simon and Schuster, 2013.

Unknown.*The Song of Roland*. tr. W.S. Merwin. Modern Library, 2001.

van Deursen, Emmy. *Everyday Mysteries*. Routledge, 1997.

von Balthasar, Hans.
– *Bernanos*. Ignatius Press, 1996.
– *The Grain of Wheat: Aphorisms*. Ignatius Press, 1995.
– *Tragedy Under Grace: Reinhold Schneider on the Experience of the West*. Ignatius, 1997.

Walker, Jeffrey. *Rhetoric and Poetics in Antiquity*. Oxford, 2000.

Wilhelmsen, Frederick D.
– *Being and Knowing*. Preserving Christian Publications, 1995.
– *Christianity and Political Philosophy*. University of Georgia, 1978.
– *Citizen of Rome*. Sherwood and Sugden, 1954.
– *Hilaire Belloc: No Alienated Man*. Sheed & Ward, 1953.

– *Man's Knowledge of Reality: An Introduction to Thomistic Episte-mology*. Prentice-Hall, 1956.

– *The Metaphysics of Love*. Sheed and Ward, 1962.

– *The Paradoxical Structure of Existence*. University of Dallas Press, 1973.

Williams, Charles. *The Last Great Frenchman: A Life of General de Gaulle*. John Wiley and Sons, 1993.

Wilson, A.N. *Hilaire Belloc*. Atheneum, 1984.

Yeats, William Butler. *Selected Poems and Two Plays*. Collier, 1962.

A Prayer

St. Michael, O Glorious One, Heavenly Physician, Standard Bearer,
Crowned with honor,
God's General,
Guide and Guardian of souls.
Direct us in our battle—Directors of Souls and Spiritual Directors,
Psychiatrists, psychologists, social workers, counselors, family therapists,
Heal us, guide us,
As we attempt to guide those who seek our counsel,
Those who suffer, those whose prayer is only to endure and to prevail,
Those who must do a soldier's service,
Those who fight the good fight, run the race, put on the armor,
Those who in pain and fear and anguish must soldier on.
Guide us, Guard us, Mighty One
As we struggle to envision,
To model strength and wisdom
To care for and about,
As You do, Comforter of Souls.
To encourage and inspire,
To be wise as the serpent
Innocent as the dove.
Give us strength and Your direction.
Give us courage
Give us heart,
So that we may inspire that gift of courage and heart in others.
Encourage, hearten us,
Pray for us O Glorious One,
St. Michael,
Prince of the Church of Jesus Christ.
Bring us to God.
We beg for your aid,
We plead for your intercession,
O Champion of the Kingdom.
Guide and Guardian of Souls.

In the name of the Father and the Son and the Holy Spirit. Amen.

www.ingramcontent.com/pod-product-compliance
Lightning Source LLC
Chambersburg PA
CBHW031507270326
41930CB00006B/289